DOGS BITE

BUT BALLOONS AND SLIPPERS ARE MORE DANGEROUS

DOGS BITE

BUT BALLOONS AND SLIPPERS ARE MORE DANGEROUS

Janis Bradley

James & Kenneth • Berkeley

Dogs Bite: But Balloons and Slippers Are More Dangerous
©2005 Janis Bradley

First published in 2005 by:

James & Kenneth Publishers
2140 Shattuck Avenue #2406
Berkeley, California 94704
1-800-784-5531

James & Kenneth—UK
Cathargoed Isaf, Golden Grove
Carmarthen, Dyfed SA32 8LY
01558-823237

James & Kenneth—OZ
P O Box 1715
Gawler SA 5116
8-8523-2004

Printed in the United States of America

ISBN 1-888047-18-6

Lisa DiPrima: illustrations for chapter headings
Jean Donaldson: photograph of Willie (opposite)
Jamie Dunbar: breed illustrations (pp. 109 and 113)
Ian Dunbar: cover photographs

For Willy

Acknowledgments

I would like to express my profound thanks to Jean Donaldson, without whose encouragement, insights, inspiration, and infinite willingness to talk about all things behavioral, this book would have remained just something I had always meant to do, and to Donald Robinson, without whose daily nagging I would never have finished it.

And thanks to the San Francisco SPCA, and to Ed Sayres and Daniel Crane in particular, for their support of this project, and to my wonderful students at the Academy for Dog Trainers for their constant inspiration.

Contents

Foreword

Humans hurt themselves in a dazzling variety of ways. For instance, in the last week, I have suffered a blister from new sandals, tripped up stairs with a laundry basket—jarring my wrist, which now aches, pinched a finger between metal plates at the gym, been bitten by an unidentified insect, had a painful hair extraction—a conspiracy between wind and the electric window in my car, bitten the inside of my mouth while eating and then proceeded to re-bite it twice more once the flesh was raised, and was attacked by thorns in my rose bushes. It'll all end when I die. I'll likely die of cancer or heart disease. If I die violently, it'll probably be in an auto wreck, or I'll fall down and it'll lead to complications. I have no doubt that dogs will be an invaluable comfort to me in my final illness. But I could also very well be bitten by one at some point. It'll make my injury list for that week.

The book you are about to read is a *tour-de-force* examination of dog bites. Among other persuasive appeals for sanity, Janis Bradley has outed "lumping": the erroneous connection between kitchen-injury level bites and maiming or fatal dog attacks. She dares to be rational. Her rationality will—hopefully—raise the level of discussion in a topic mired in hysteria.

Why *do* we get so excited about this particular class of injury? Enter the irrational. Human brains are organs that evolved for a single over-arching purpose: to maximize the representation of genes possessed by an individual brain's owner in subsequent generations. We evolved in a different environment than the one we currently inhabit, however. Because of this, we are genetically predisposed to learn to fear animals with pointy teeth much more than to fear, say, hurtling along in hunks of metal at sixty-five miles per hour.

Our brains are also not reliable truth detection devices. Any instances of truth detection are lucky by-products of selection for reproductive success. Scientific method was developed because of the chronic, abysmal failure of our brains to dope out reality, coupled with a fascination to know truth. Our intuitions are flat-footed much of the time. Stephen Jay Gould once mused, "the invalid assumption that correlation implies cause is probably among the two or three most serious and common errors of human reasoning."

If one searches the backgrounds of that small minority of dogs that kill people, lo and behold, many of them will have previously engaged in species-normal ritualized aggression: growls, snarls and kitchen-injury or less level bites in predictable contexts. This then becomes the foundation for the faulty causal leap, a slippery slope argument that says: if a dog is growly around his food dish, he will someday seriously hurt or kill someone. What is omitted is that a significant percentage of all dogs engage in species-normal ritualized aggression and the overwhelming majority will never hurt, much less kill, anyone.

A significant percentage (I guess close to one hundred) of people will argue in their lifetimes but this is not a flag for subsequent felony assault. If this book does no more than raise awareness of the difference between arguing and assault in dogs—and I suspect it will do much more—it will have done a great thing.

Jean Donaldson
August 28, 2005

14

The Big Picture

D ogs are dangerous. And they are more dangerous to children than to adults. Not as dangerous, of course, as front-porch steps or kitchen utensils or five-gallon water buckets or bathtubs or strollers or stoves or lamp cords or coffee-table corners or Christmas trees or balloons or bedroom slippers. Not nearly as dangerous as playground equipment or skateboards or bikes or baseballs or soccer fields or parked cars or swimming pools. And obviously, dogs can never compete as hazards with fathers or mothers or sisters or brothers or aunts or uncles or friends or guns or cars.

Still, dogs have big pointed teeth that they can bring together faster than the human eye can follow, applying hundreds of pounds of pressure to puncture and tear. And sometimes they use some of this power on human flesh.

So states and municipalities pass dangerous dog statutes, plaintiffs are awarded enormous sums for dog-related injuries, insurance companies refuse homeowner's coverage to many dog owners and many landlords won't rent to them, while many dogs are killed. It's time to consider whether any of this makes sense.

Here's the reality. Dogs almost never kill people. A child is more likely to die choking on a balloon or falling off a swing than being bitten by a dog. The supposed epidemic numbers of dog bites cited in the media are absurdly inflated by questionable research techniques and by counting the bites that don't actually hurt anyone. Even when dogs do injure people, the vast majority of dog bite injuries are at the Band-Aid level.

Why all the alarm? Partly because our own evolution has programmed us to be more scared of predators (think saber toothed tigers) than of machines (think cars) and partly because stories about things with big teeth keep us tuned to Channel 4 better than stories about things with big wheels and a couple of tons of fast moving metal.

But what makes dogs dogs is that they like people better as companions than as lunch. Their immediate ancestors, wolves, don't like people at all, and saber toothed tigers were, I presume, of the lunch persuasion. People sometimes compromise this doggy friendliness by breeding for more hostility, but they're bucking the tide of millennia of canine evolution.

Dogs do fairly often get irritated enough with us to growl or snarl or snap, although far less frequently than we engage in the human equivalents of making snide remarks, arguing, and yelling. Dogs share with us some of the common triggers for such irritation, like possessiveness, self-defense, and the urge to protect offspring. But they tip over into actual violence in resolving conflicts less readily than do we.

Much of the effort put into studying which dogs are most likely to bite has been wasted on looking at incidence by breed. Breed characteristics are driven by fashion and change too quickly, and breed identification is too unreliable for this to yield any useful information. Even the few well designed studies on growling, snarling, snapping, and biting in dogs have so far failed to unearth any connections with these behaviors that go beyond the scope of the rawest common sense.

Legislatures respond to this flawed research and the media frenzy surrounding dog bites with laws that have no hope of decreasing dog bites. The worst of these are the breed bans which get a lot of dogs killed but do nothing to deter criminals who conduct dogfights and deliberately breed neophobic dogs. Insurance companies jump in by denying homeowner's insurance to many dog owners, perhaps with an eye to exploiting people's paranoia about lawsuits with a whole new liability insurance product.

Meanwhile, the companionship of tens of millions of dogs quietly benefits many times more people than even the most inflated estimates of dog bite victims. Infants who live with dogs in the first year of life have fewer allergies. People with dogs have lower cardiovascular disease risk, and are more likely to survive heart attacks if they do occur. Petting your dog lowers stress. Dogs facilitate social contact, and people who live with dogs just plain feel better than people who don't.

If we want to maintain these enormous benefits there will always be some dog bites. However, there are some steps that may reasonably be expected to decrease injuries. We can teach kids to behave in ways that don't set off the more common aggression triggers in dogs, and while we're at it, adults can be taught to act sensibly around dogs, too. We can breed only those dogs who are relaxed when people mess around with their stuff and who are friendly with strangers. We can carefully socialize puppies to all manner of potentially scary situations and teach them to use their teeth gently when they are upset enough to bite.

To accomplish all this, however, we must give up the pernicious view of dogs as personal bodyguards who can tell the difference between good guys and bad guys. Instead, we can celebrate them as comforters and companions who enrich the quality of our lives. This is a job for education, not legislation.

And such public education should include a clear eyed looked at the facts which are: dogs almost never kill people, they bite much less often than one would expect, and when they bite, they seldom injure.

CHAPTER ONE

Dog Bites: Big Danger or Cultural Phobia?

In my favorite scene in the movie Moonstruck, when the mother's philandering husband walks into the house late one evening, she greets him with, "You know, Cosmo, no matter what you do, you're gonna die just like everybody else." She's been busily quizzing every man she meets about why men chase women, looking for comfort and for confirmation of her theory that it's because they fear death. Cosmo doesn't pause on his way up the stairs as he responds, "Thank you, Rose, I'm going to bed."

Would that we could all be so matter of fact, because, of course, Rose is right. Each of us faces one in one odds of dying. But it's not going to be a dog that kills you. I mean this literally. Even if this book skyrockets to the top of the New York Times Best-Seller List and stays there for months, these words will not be read by enough people to have a serious chance of including one who is killed by a dog.

19

Fatal Dog Attacks Are Fantastically Rare

Your chances of being killed by a dog or dogs are roughly one in 18 million. That means you are twice as likely to win a super lotto jackpot on a single ticket than to be killed by a dog. That means you are five times as likely to be killed by a bolt of lightning—not just struck by one, mind you—killed. It's instructive to remember here that being struck by lightning is a pretty universal cliché for an act of God being visited upon one, precisely because it is so extraordinary. Dog-attack deaths are even more extraordinary— five times more extraordinary.

Figure 1. Very Rare Causes of Accidental Deaths

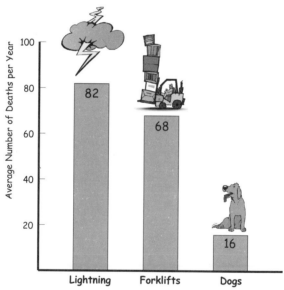

Dog bites are among the rarest of fatal mishaps. For every person who dies as a result of dog bites, five are killed by lightning. For every dog bite fatality, four people are killed by forklifts, even though a very small number of people actually come into contact with these machines.
Annual data based on averaging fatalities for 10–15 year CDC sponsored studies of individual cases.

20

There are scores of variables in any dog-human interaction. A great many of them must go astonishingly wrong all in one direction and all at the same time to produce a dog bite fatality, rather like a perfect storm. Such events are extraordinary in the most literal sense: far, far outside of the ordinary. This is why they are so rare and why it's not much use to look for trends among them.

One point that is made over and over, however, and so should probably be addressed, is that more children and old people die from dog bites than people from their teens through middle age. It's true that an able-bodied adult is virtually never (about twice per decade) killed by a single dog. The small proportion of fatalities among people between the ages of 11 and 64 usually involve multiple dogs. Yes, dogs do kill more children than adults. However, dog bite fatalities fall far behind other very rare causes of death in children, including five-gallon buckets, party balloons, and swings,

Figure 2 gives a sense of the relative risks. Another much more common cause of childhood fatalities, caregiver abuse, is added to give some idea of scale. Of course, the scale is deceptive, because in order to accurately represent the rate of abuse fatalities, the bar would go off the page. In fact it would stretch eleven pages beyond this graph.

What no one points out, of course, as they frown solemnly and intone that something must be done, is that, babies, children, and old people are more likely to die of mishaps in general: compared with teenagers and middle-aged adults: they are weaker, more fragile, react more slowly and less efficiently, and are smaller.

21

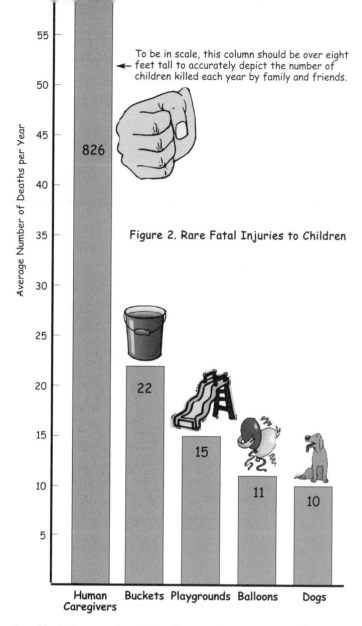

To be in scale, this column should be over eight feet tall to accurately depict the number of children killed each year by family and friends.

Figure 2. Rare Fatal Injuries to Children

Average Number of Deaths per Year

826

22

15

11

10

Human Caregivers | Buckets | Playgrounds | Balloons | Dogs

Toys like balloons and marbles, playground equipment, and five gallon buckets each cause more fatalities every year to children under 10 than do dogs. Caregiver (mostly family member) physical abuse fatalities are included to show the scale of this much more serious threat to children. Annual data based on averaging fatalities from separate 10–15 year CDC sponsored studies of individual cases.

22

Children are more likely than adults to suffer fatal injuries in bicycle accidents, for example. Children under 14 have the highest fatality rate from accidental injuries (other than car accidents) of any age group.

At the other end of the life span, the elderly have their own vulnerabilities. Old bones often fracture more easily than do younger ones, for one thing. Combine this with a higher rate of mobility and equilibrium problems among the elderly, and it's easy to see how this population segment is at high risk for falls and sustains more serious injuries when they do fall.

You can't even make a visually accurate chart comparing dog-bite risk with these other, enormously more serious, hazards. Making the bar representing dog-bite fatalities high enough to see in Figure 3 is impossible.

As a teacher of people who aspire to become professional dog trainers at an institution dedicated to fostering the human-animal bond, I spend my entire professional life working to promote safe, happy, harmonious relationships between dogs and humans. And the first of these concerns is always safety. Yet when people ask me what I think should be done to prevent dog-bite deaths, I'm always tempted to answer, "Nothing."

This is partly because the question strikes me as so bizarre. We certainly accept the idea that as long as we use cars, some people will die in them, that as long as we have medicines, some people will have fatal reactions to them, that as long as we have bathtubs and shower stalls, some people will slip and fracture their skulls in them.

DOGS BITE: BUT BALLOONS AND SLIPPERS ARE MORE DANGEROUS

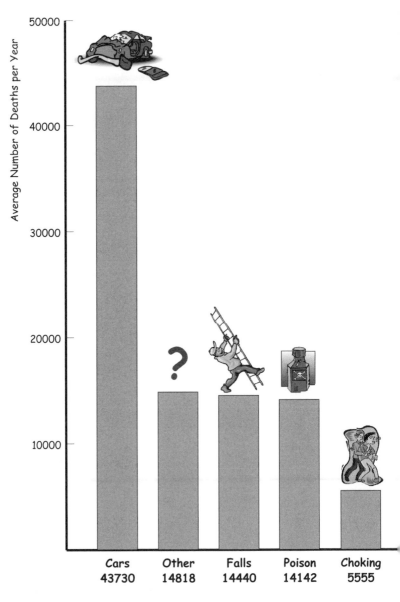

Average Number of Deaths per Year

Cars	Other	Falls	Poison	Choking
43730	14818	14440	14142	5555

24

Figure 3. Accidental Deaths

Figure 3 represents the numbers of unintentional injury deaths from different causes annually for all age groups. Annual dog bite deaths are estimated from a separate 10-year study as they are too rare to be captured in CDC injury fatality data. Obviously, the small annual number dog bite deaths cannot be accurately depicted in this graph.

Data Source: Center for Disease Control and Prevention. Web-based Injury Statistics Query and Reporting System (WISGARS) for 1999–2002.

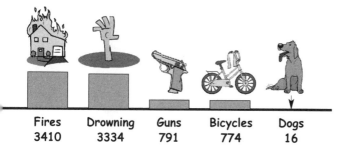

Fires	Drowning	Guns	Bicycles	Dogs
3410	3334	791	774	16

We take as many precautions as seem to us reasonable to prevent these events, but no one seriously expects to reduce them to zero. And certainly no one stops driving, taking medicine when they get sick, or bathing, because of these hazards. If they do, we consider them to be suffering from clinical phobias and try to get them medical and psychiatric treatment.

We may well be as close to zero as it is possible to get in terms of dog-bite death risk. The risk is so small that there are actually three states where there has not been a single recorded dog bite death in four decades. This does not mean that if you want to avoid being killed by a dog, you should move to Iowa or North Dakota or Rhode Island. It means that these events are so vanishingly rare as to be, for all practical purposes, random.

More people, more dogs, same number of dog bite deaths

The rate of dog-bite deaths has remained very steady for decades despite changes in practically every aspect of the human-dog enterprise. The human population has increased significantly, without doubt resulting in a net increase in dog to human contacts. Relative popularity of various breeds has been in a constant state of flux, almost certainly including a sizable increase in the numbers among the so-called dangerous breeds.

The ways we share our lives with dogs have changed dramatically, mainly in a trend away from backyard solitary confinement of dogs and toward more incorporation into households, and more exposure to the outside world, including exponential increases in dog-to-dog contacts. In other words, practically everything we might expect to affect the rate of dog-bite fatalities has been altered in some way over this period of time, and still the rate of these events has not increased.

Lassie or Cujo? Nobody Knows

Moreover, many of the conditions surrounding dog-bite deaths appear likely to simply reflect the distributions of events in dog's lives. More bites (75 percent) happen in the dogs' own homes, for example, but most dogs spend more time at home than away. More bites involve people known to the dog, but dogs see more familiar people than strangers. And so on.

We are very, very far from identifying factors (or more likely intricate combinations of factors) that every once in a very great while happen to come together to produce one of these freakish events. It's difficult to make a case for the resource expenditure it would take to even try, especially given the competition for resources to study phenomena that result in far more human deaths and serious injuries, from pandemic infectious diseases to guns and cars.

We think, of course, that we know a lot about dogs. We don't. We definitely don't know which dogs are going to hurt people and under what circumstances. When you consider the sheer numbers of canines living among us, the paucity of actual observational studies of domestic dogs is pretty surprising, just from the perspective of scientific curiosity. The reality is that we have at present no reliable data that would allow us to predict with any measure of certainty (or even anything much beyond chance), that any particular dog who has not already done so is more likely to deliver a damaging bite than any other dog, either in terms of genetics or of past behavior, or of the life circumstances of the animal.

There are some data on these questions, but all of it is highly suspect for various reasons. There are lots of hypotheses (talk to any group of two or more dog professionals for a dizzying array of often contradictory examples). Some of us may well be correct in our theories, but we don't know who we are.

The Butterfly Effect, Canine Style

We do know something about canine warning signals—growls and snarls and snaps, and more subtly, freezes and a fixed stare commonly called, "hard eye." These are the dog's way of saying, "please don't make me bite you." In a small percentage of the cases when such signals are not heeded, they culminate in bites. A very small proportion of the bites are forceful enough to injure.

We know something about the kinds of interactions with humans that can elicit these warning signals. This knowledge gives us a place to start (pending better research on actual biting dogs), to try to reduce the number of growls and snarls and snaps directed at people.

But even if we implement this knowledge and the majority of people cooperate (a long shot, since not everyone involved with dogs actually wants to reduce dog aggression) it's entirely possible that this will have no effect whatsoever on the rate of fatalities, precisely because these are so incredibly rare.

But, "Ah," people say, "Even one life lost is too many." We must do whatever it takes to prevent this. No one disputes that these are horrific events. But what would it take? Short of eliminating all dogs in order to get rid of the approximately one dog in about five million that is involved in a fatal attack each year, we simply don't know how to prevent these incidents. Nor are we ever likely to know, as the population of dogs that kill people will never be large enough to support meaningful generalizations.

Basic systems theory teaches us that it is perilous to change the system to eradicate the exception, and dog-bite deaths are about as exceptional as it gets. It is perilous because when you change large-scale situations to prevent extremely rare events, you cannot even begin to predict what other aberrant, or even widespread, events may pop up. Eliminating all dogs to prevent fatal attacks is an obvious example. It's easy to see how this could result in far more deaths among those helped by service dogs alone, or those found by search and rescue dogs, not to mention the millions whose lives are extended by the improvement in general health and well being conferred by sharing one's life with a dog.

Let's examine a seemingly more feasible intervention, since we're no more likely to eliminate all dogs to prevent 15 fatalities than we are to ban bicycles to prevent 740 deaths or cars to prevent 43,000.

Some dog-bite fatalities appear to involve group predatory behavior (see Peter Borchelt's article for an analysis of two harrowing cases of groups of roaming dogs chasing down a bicyclist and a jogger). This could be prevented by cracking down on people who allow their dogs to roam. Such a crackdown might even reduce the gross number of dog bites over all.

However, law-enforcement resources would have to be pulled from preventing and responding to other kinds of threats to public safety. How many life-saving interventions would they miss? Moreover, some dogs are more likely to bite when confined than when free to retreat. If two or three such dogs caught in the anti-roaming dragnet happened to coincide with some combination of factors that lead to fatal bites to familiar people, the overall fatality rates would remain the same. And yet every time a fatal (or near fatal) dog-bite incident screams its way across the headlines, there's an immediate outcry for some way to legislate away the terrible menace.

As if anyone knew how.

It's worth gathering the facts and engaging in careful consideration before we jump into any sweeping changes in an attempt to decrease dog bites. We might easily make things worse, since the reality now is that dogs almost never kill people, and they don't actually bite very often, and when they do, we're seldom injured, and when we are, it's seldom serious.

CHAPTER TWO

Dog Bites—Big Numbers—Or Are They?

My youngest brother, Craig, when he was about seven, sobbed uncontrollably in my mother's arms for the better part of an afternoon, certain he'd be torn away from us and taken up to heaven at any moment after he bumped into the fender of a barely moving car while riding his bike. He was unhurt, but he had been so scrupulously warned about the dangers of cars to bicyclists that he was convinced that any collision with a car would certainly be fatal. When he finally settled down and discovered that he wasn't dead, however, he was able to go on to ride his bike around the neighborhood with reasonable caution instead of terror.

The people who study the epidemiology of dog bite fatalities could take a lesson from Craig's experience. They dutifully acknowledge the rarity of these events, but then quickly shift their mournful attention to the nonfatal bites. Phrases like "growing public health crisis" and words like "epidemic" are never far behind.

31

Everybody Knows Things Are Getting Worse
—How Six Turns Into Half A Million

These alarmist claims are supported mainly by two big numbers from two National Center for Injury Prevention and Control surveys, one done in 1986, the other in 1994. The analysis from the second survey is quoted everywhere. It supposedly shows a 36-percent increase in medically treated dog bites by comparing the 1994 totals with those from 1986. However, both numbers are deeply flawed. Comparing them to each other is plainly absurd.

In the 1986 survey, six injurious dog bites were reported. Members of 23,838 households were queried about injuries that had resulted in "restricted activity" or medical treatment for any member of the household during the two weeks preceding the survey. (The researchers also asked about injuries occurring during the preceding 12 months, but found people's recollection beyond two weeks to be so unreliable that they excluded these data from their results.) So the study included a total of 62,052 people. Among the falls and car wrecks and bicycle accidents and spider bites, the interviewees reported just six dog bites. These six bites were used to come up with a national figure of 585,000 bites for the year. No really, six.

When you start extrapolating into the hundreds of thousands based on something you didn't need all your fingers, much less your toes, to count, things get pretty, shall we say, hinky. You don't need to review the Introduction to your Statistics textbook to recognize this. The researchers themselves said as much, pointing out that all but the three most common causes of injuries (falls, automobile accidents, and drug mishaps) had large margins of error.

In other words, don't expect a similar result even if you call another 23,838 people selected in exactly the same way and ask

32

them exactly the same questions the very next day (more on this in Chapter Six). To compare the results of such a study with one conducted differently is statistically ludicrous.

Yet this is exactly what the 1994 study, the one cited everywhere to support the "alarming increase" in dog bites idea, did. They interviewed only a fraction as many people (5,328 vs. 23,838). They asked about bites over a whole year's time (a practice the first study had concluded was extremely unreliable). Only one adult and one child from each household were included for a total of 8,869 people. Injurious was defined differently. Finally, the study asked only about dog bites, rather than embedding this in a much more wide ranging interview covering all injuries.

The subjects reported 38 dog bite injuries. At least this required the digits of two researchers to tally. The authors extrapolated this to 756,701, in their ambitiously titled article, Dog Bites: How Big A Problem? At least they included a question mark.

The researchers blithely claim that this difference demonstrates a "36-percent increase" in medically treated bites in the 12 years between the two studies. Interestingly, this claim is only implied in the report itself, but explicitly made in another study with the same lead author on the subject of fatal dog attacks. Once these authors began citing themselves in the fatality study, the injurious bite number rose to the conveniently rounded total of 800,000. This included estimates of bites to 15- to 17-year-olds, who were not even included in the survey.

As you might imagine, insurance companies and personal-injury lawyers have had a tremendously good time with this bogus comparison. More on this in Chapter Nine. But they're not the only

33

ones. You find the study cited by everyone from humane societies to child-safety organizations. The results of these flawed studies are picked up and chanted so frequently by other respectable sources that their statistics gain credence simply though repetition, and away we go on the "public-health crisis" ride.

Is It A Public Health Problem When No One Is Hurt?

It gets worse. Bites that injured people were not the main focus of the "how big a problem?" study. They wanted to count all dog bites, not just those that hurt anybody. The 5,328 interviewees reported 186 bites among the 8,869 people covered by the survey. The researchers concluded that 4,494,083 people had been bitten nationwide that year. This is pretty much the same order of magnitude that brought us the transformation of six actual injurious bites into half a million from the 1986 injury survey.

The "how gig" people then threw in the 215,600 bites they believed they "would have detected" had they included 15- to 17-year-olds in the survey. Voilà, here is the source of the 4.7 million annual dog bites that is bandied about across the literature. But the unreliability of the numbers is still not the biggest issue here.

The amazing thing is that anybody would try to count events that don't hurt anybody as part of a public health study. These guys counted 148 of them, which they extrapolated to mean that 3,737,382 people were bitten by dogs that year, but were unscathed. This, according to the study, ought to be a cause of great concern.

This is an absolutely extraordinary idea, that events which cause no harm should be counted as part of a public-health problem. No

34

one even thinks to try to track how many times people trip and fall, for example, or how many times they drop a paring knife making salad for dinner, or touch a stove that isn't lit, or are approached by a bee that doesn't sting, or bump into something with a bike, unless the person is hurt. Try remembering such events in your own life, even over a short period, and you'll soon give it up as hopeless. They're just too trivial to make the memory radar.

Not only are we uninterested in counting these non-injury events, nobody bothers counting injuries below a certain level of severity, usually ones for which medical attention is required. One can reasonably assume, for example, that something close to 100 percent of kids fall off their trikes and bikes multiple times without injury, and that most have probably sustained a skinned elbow or knee from time to time.

The same can surely be said for taking spills off playground equipment and skateboards, touching a still-hot pan to the point of an "ouch," but not a burn, nicking themselves with a paring knife helping to make salad for dinner. We take some precautions to prevent these mundane events, but since they are such everyday occurrences, we put more energy into preventing them from resulting in injuries when they do occur. Certainly, no one would see any sense in trying to count them. If they did, of course, the numbers would obviously be enormous.

So let's for the moment suspend the credibility difficulties with the 4.7 million bites per year. If this happens to be accurate, it means that every human who lives to the age of 60 in the United States can reasonably expect to be bitten by a dog at least once. (Based on a total US population of around 290 million.) Or for everyone

35

DOGS BITE: BUT BALLOONS AND SLIPPERS ARE MORE DANGEROUS

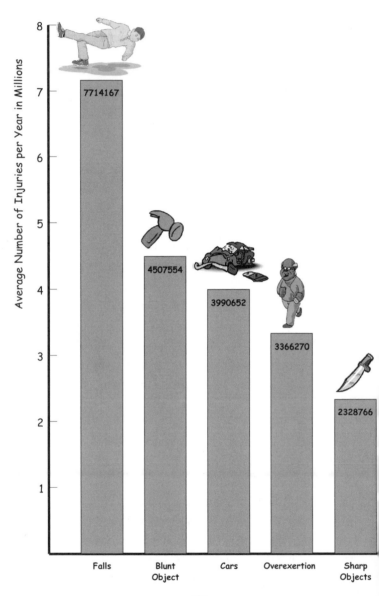

ure 4. Accidental Injuries Treated in Emergency Departments

Average annual injuries treated in Emergency Departments from 2001–2003. Sports related injuries (4.3 million) are distributed mainly among falls, blunt objects, and overexertion categories.

Data Source: Center for Disease Control and Prevention. Web-based Injury Statistics Query and Reporting System (WISGARS).

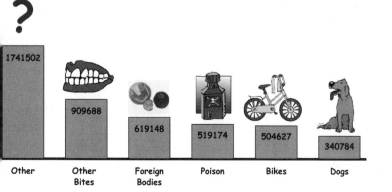

Other	Other Bites	Foreign Bodies	Poison	Bikes	Dogs
1741502	909688	619148	519174	504627	340784

who isn't bitten, some other poor soul must be taking his bite. At first glance, it makes you wonder why people would want to have dogs around at all. Then you consider that according to the study's own calculations, roughly 3,900,000 of bites don't actually hurt the bitees.

People keep dogs, of course, because they're pleasant company and seldom hurt us. Yet even benign tooth-related events are referred to with frowny solemnity everywhere in the media and professional literature. This seems quite significant with respect to our attitude toward dog bites. No one even attempts to study similar phenomena when they don't produce physical harm. With regard to dog bites, we seem to have major confusion between a type of event, which is harmless 80 to 90 percent of the time, and the injury itself.

"Ashes, Ashes, All Fall Down"

Nevertheless, it is safe to say that dog bites occur relatively frequently, like skinned knees and stubbed toes, and tripping and falling down, although once again, not nearly as frequently as any of these. Not frequently, of course, by the kind of standards used to tabulate risk (rate of occurrence per unit of exposure time, for example). Not frequently when you use the common sense measure of the estimated 60 to 64 million dogs in this country, or one for every four to five people, with most of those dogs coming into contact with several people (at least) every day, resulting in tens of billions of hours (conservatively) of dog-human contact every year.

Almost anything with that kind of massive exposure is going to carry some hazards. For example, roughly 180 million people of all ages in the US participate in some kind of sport or physical activity at least occasionally. The actual exposure time is probably much lower than that with dogs, but at least it's a large scale one. So about double the number of people who live with dogs participate in sports. Yet emergency departments treat over 13 times as many sports-related injuries as dog bites.

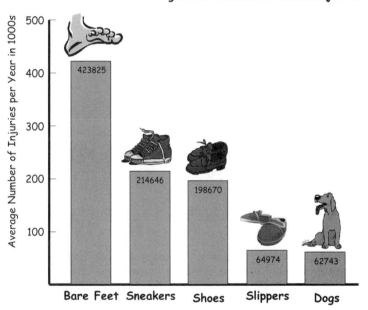

Figure 5. Footwear Related Injuries

You need look no farther than your closet floor for hazards more pressing than your dog. In the United Kingdom, where injuries are broken down by very specific causes, bedroom slippers and sneakers each cause significantly more medically treated injuries than dogs. This is also true for "other" shoes, which do not include slippers, sneakers, sandals, high heels, platforms, clogs, or boots. And you can't avoid the danger by going barefoot, which is almost twice as dangerous as any kind of footware.
Data Source: Royal Society for the Prevention of Accidents, Home and Leisure Accident Surveillance System. Annual Report 2000–2002

To take a more whimsical example, we might consider the bedroom slipper menace. In the UK, where they tracked agents of accidental injuries in detail through 2002, bedroom slipper injuries are slightly more common than dog-related ones (which include mishaps other than bites). And injuries resulting from going barefoot? More than twice as many.

Figure 6. Furniture Dangers

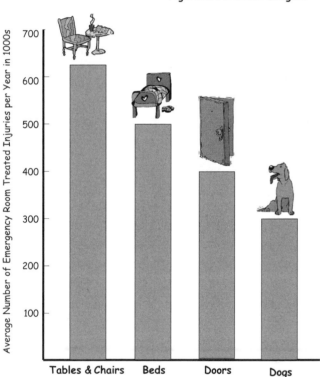

Tables are responsible for roughly the same number of emergency room treated injuries per year as dog bites, as are chairs. So the whole dining set is almost twice as hazardous. Beds and doors are also significantly more dangerous than dogs, so if you thought you were safe shutting the bedroom door and pulling the covers over your head, think again Data Source: US Consumer Product Safety Commission: NEISS data for 2003.

Dogs Versus Swing Sets

Odd comparisons are sometimes made between dog-bite-caused injuries and other causes, particularly injuries that affect children. One major study on dog-bite-related fatalities done for the National Center for Injury Prevention and Control, for example, describes the 12–15 fatalities and 368,000 emergency-room (ER) visits among all age groups annually for dog bites as "similar" to the17 fatalities, and 205,000 ER visits among children alone for playground equipment accidents. (The article uses somewhat different figures, but these are the actual numbers from the studies cited.)

One of several important points they neglect to mention is the massive difference in exposure rates between the two phenomena. The dog bite figures cover the entire population, from infants through the elderly. On the other hand, children under 14 make up only about 21 percent of the total population and account for virtually all playground injuries. Thus a much smaller segment of the population is actually exposed to the playground equipment risk, and even that exposure is probably less frequent and of less duration than this same population's exposure to dogs. It seems very unlikely that there are 60 million pieces of playground equipment in the US (this would be more than one for every kid in the country under the age of 12 at the time of this writing).

But the real elephant in the living room here is this—almost half (45 percent) of playground injuries are severe by one authoritative estimate. They are internal injuries, concussions, dislocated, fractured, and amputated limbs. More than three percent of children in ER's for playground accidents are hospitalized. Most dog-bite injuries are minor punctures and lacerations. Between 1 and 1.6 percent of ER-treated–dog-bite victims are admitted to hospitals for treatment or observation, according to three different studies tracking hospitalizations. This spurious incidence comparison is then used to support the complaint that the dog-bite problem has not enjoyed a similar prevention effort compared to the playground injury problem which has produced standards for equipment and playgrounds, training and inspection programs, dedication of staff to maintenance, and, most recently, the creation of a federally-funded national center for playground safety to educate the public (Sacks, et. al., 1996).

Figure 7. Fatal Injuries to Children 10 Years and Younger

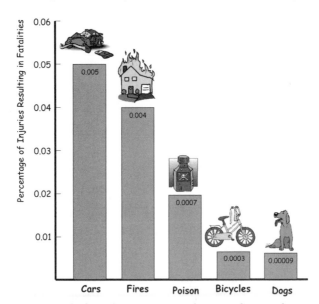

One way to look at the seriousness of injuries by specific cause is to consider how frequently a type of injury is fatal. This chart shows the proportion of those injuries to children (less than 10 years of age) serious enough to be treated in ER, that proved to be fatal. The highest rate (far left) shows that one in 179 car accident victims taken to an ER dies. One in 10,995 dog bite victims taken to hospital dies of those injuries.
Data Sources: CDC and WISGARS for 2001–2002. Dog bite fatality data from CDC studies, 1979–1998.

Dogs—As Regulated As Guns

In fact, however, domestic dogs are substantially regulated. No one is required to register the backyard swing set they purchase at the local discount warehouse, even though backyard equipment accounts for the majority of fatalities. In contrast, virtually every community in the country requires registration of dogs, including proof of immunization. This is a major example of developing and implementing a safety standard for dogs. It has resulted in the eradication of a once-real danger of dog bites to humans: rabies infection. Once a fairly regular occurrence, there has not been a single documented case of human rabies contracted from a domestic dog in the United States since 1979. (There is a very occasional case of a domestic dog contracting rabies, but this is readily contained.)

Equally widespread are requirements that dogs be confined, either on the owner's property, or on a leash in public, except for designated (and often hotly contested) public areas. Certainly the enforcement of these regulations is often spotty, but this is not evidence of lack of regulatory attention to the issue.

Attempts to establish something analogous to general safety standards for dogs have been enacted by countless communities. These are in reaction, usually, to isolated high-profile bite cases. They have been very problematic in their conclusions, often resulting in grotesquely flawed policies like breed bans (more on this in Chapter 6). Sometimes the legislative bodies are just flying by the seat of their pants; sometimes they cite the irresponsibly flawed studies that pass for research in this field, but so called "dangerous-dog" laws undeniably exist.

Yelling Is Not The Same As Assault With A Deadly Weapon
Most attempts to eliminate "dangerous dogs," however, spring from a completely erroneous premise. They are based on the belief that the dog that has bitten, or even growled or snarled or snapped, whether or not he has done harm, is much more likely to deliver a wounding bite than one who has not bitten. Supposedly, the dog has somehow demonstrated his bad character. This is completely unproven conjecture. Whether a dog will growl or snarl or snap is the wrong question. Most dogs will. This is what dogs do when they are upset. The right question is whether the dog will actually hurt anybody.

Growling, snarling, and snapping are warning signals, the dog's way of saying, "Back off." Quite often, these signals do persuade people to retreat, and thus prevent bites. Certainly, the dog that is uncomfortable enough around humans to want to drive them away is an urgent candidate for behavior modification, but the dog that does not signal his discomfort with growls or snarls or snaps is far more dangerous. This is the animal that bites without warning.

In any case, no matter how affiliative, well socialized and tolerant a dog is, there is simply no guarantee that he will go though his life without ever having an upsetting encounter with a human. Most do have such encounters. The most critical question is what the dog does when he is upset enough to bite. What does he do when the toddler sticks a finger in his eye or grabs his precious meaty bone? The study of the social behavior of the dog's closest relative, the wolf, and of domestic dogs has something to say about this.

As predators, wolves and dogs have formidable weapons capable of killing prey. As social animals, however, who often depend on the solidarity of their extended family groups for mutual protection and for cooperative hunting, they need a way to live together and resolve conflicts among themselves with a minimum of damage to one another. How do they do this?

Dr. Frank Beach and Dr. Ian Dunbar conducted a nearly decade-long study of a dog colony (one of only two such studies of domestic dogs ever done), at the University of California at Berkeley in the 1970's. They observed that, like wolves, as these dogs grew up among their conspecifics, they learned to moderate the pressure of their jaws on one another, even in the midst of quite heated confrontations. The pups learned during play and scuffling that if they applied too much pressure with their needle like little teeth, their playmates would shriek the puppy version of "Ouch!" and stop playing. Having to suspend playtime while your partner grumbles and licks his "wounds" is a powerful punishment indeed for such a profoundly social animal.

Thus puppies learn to bite gently without injuring. It's quite possible that our most effective route to fewer dog bite injuries would be to focus on breeding and training dogs for ease of acquisition and reliability of this behavior, called acquired bite inhibition. An adult dog with a history of snaps, nips and bites with no injuries is arguably more demonstrably safe than even the most tolerant animal. Every dog has a breaking point.

Focusing on installing bite inhibition would be much more analogous to the approach taken with regard to playground equipment safety, where no one anticipates eliminating falls off the equipment. Everyone expects kids to fall. The goal is to have them fall without getting hurt. This is done mostly by modifying the equipment. Bite inhibition is much like the rubber padding underneath the jungle gym. The results are bites and falls that don't hurt anyone.

My docile Greyhound, Henry, screamed and thrashed in a panic one day when he caught his toe in a blanket. I was quite pleased when as I attempted to free his foot, he bit me quickly three times. I was pleased because although I saw his jaws on my wrist. I didn't feel his teeth at all. It is very reassuring to see that his gentle mouth holds up even in a state of panic.

Some attention can also paid, of course, to teaching children to behave as safely as possible, and to thus fall off the jungle gym and upset the dog less often. Something like this latter approach (of teaching kids about basic safety around dogs) will be discussed in the final chapter, as it might have some effect in reducing the number of bites, injurious and non injurious.

Help! Help! That Dog's Tooth Scratched Me!

But let's look at how we respond when there actually is an injury. My dog Willy once bit a cop who approached and reached for him suddenly when the dog walker had him out one evening. When he's on leash, strangers rushing up and reaching for him, uniforms, and nighttime each make him a bit nervous—the combination was too much. Willy jumped up, and probably with one of his long canine teeth, made a three inch tear in the cop's shirt and scratched the top of his forearm. There was no contact with the underside of the arm. Willy had either scratched the top in passing while grabbing the shirt, or put his mouth around the arm without closing it, demonstrating admirable bite inhibition. It was decided that no Band-Aid was needed.

The officer's response to this event, however, was, "Wow, he really nailed me, didn't he?" Now Willy was in his prime at the time of this incident, an athletic, 100-pound Rottweiler/German Shepherd mix. He would not have needed the full pressure of his jaws for more than a split second to break the man's arm. And even though this happened in a tiny town in Marin County where the most dangerous situation the police force ever faces is breaking up the occasional bar fight, the cop, presumably, would have been too macho to even acknowledge an injury of this lack of severity in any other context.

But let's say my dog walker had been less level-headed, and instead of steadying the officer with a, "Now, come on, that doesn't look like much of a bite," had supported his exaggerated response. I doubt he would have taken much convincing to "seek medical attention," the usual gold standard of serious injuries. I have long suspected that many people perceive injuries from dog bites through a different lens (possibly a magnifying glass) than the one they use for injuries from other ordinary causes.

More Band-Aids Than Sutures

In fact the data on ER and hospital treatment for dog bites bear out this suspicion. As a class of injury receiving medical treatment, dog bites, on average, are less severe (according to the accepted measurement, called an injury severity scale) than any other class of common injury. The average treated dog bite is rated as minor, at the lowest level, 1 out of 6. (A level 1 injury is one from which the person recovers quickly with no lasting impairment; a level 6 is one likely to be fatal.) Only one percent of all treated bites rate as more severe than level 1.

47

Figure 8. Severity of Dog Bite Injuries

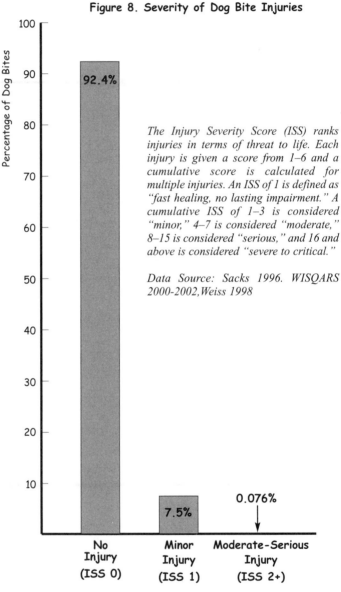

The Injury Severity Score (ISS) ranks injuries in terms of threat to life. Each injury is given a score from 1–6 and a cumulative score is calculated for multiple injuries. An ISS of 1 is defined as "fast healing, no lasting impairment." A cumulative ISS of 1–3 is considered "minor," 4–7 is considered "moderate," 8–15 is considered "serious," and 16 and above is considered "severe to critical."

Data Source: Sacks 1996. WISQARS 2000-2002,Weiss 1998

To place this in perspective, ER treatment for falls averages around a 4. This is a moderate injury, meaning one which either requires weeks to months to fully heal or results in lasting minor impairment. This comparison between fall and dog bite injury severity is based on studies of each injury modality conducted by the Pennsylvania Department of Health in 1994 and 1995. These studies were used as they were both products of the same data source, compiled in the same way, and covering all relevant hospital discharges (not samples) for the year.

Compared to people treated for dog bites, people treated for falls are four times as likely to be admitted to the hospital and over 100 times more likely to die of their injuries. This discrepancy holds true for other injuries as well. Year after year, according to national data, even injuries from overexertion are more severe (and more common) than those from dog bites.

As one would expect from this, the average treatment for dog bites costs less and results in lengthy hospitalization far less frequently than other causes of injury.

This helps explain why kids who have been bitten are no more scared of dogs than kids who haven't. This at-first-glance puzzling finding was made in the context of a frequently cited 1980 Pennsylvania study of about 3,200 school children. 46 percent of the kids reported having been bitten hard enough to leave a scratch at some time in their lives. They still liked dogs just as well as the kids who hadn't been bitten. In all likelihood, closer to 100 percent of them had fallen off their bikes and skinned their knees. They probably still liked bikes, too.

In the above study, there is some question as to how many of the children surveyed were actually given the instruction to report only bites that had broken skin, and had been aggressive, rather

Figure 9. Comparative Severity of Dog Bites vs. Falls

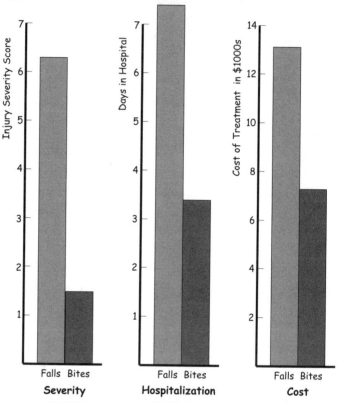

Even for causes that require hospitalization, dog bite injuries are much less severe than those from falls. Hospital treatment for dog bites, on the rare occasions that it is needed, costs less than that for falls and does not last as long, requiring only half the hospital stay on average.

A cumulative Injury Severity Score (ISS) of 1–3 is considered "minor," 4–7 "moderate," 8–15 "serious," and 16+ "life threatening."

Data Source: Pennsylvania Department of Health, Injury Profiles monographs, 1994 and 1995.

than "playful." Thus some that resulted in not even this slight level of injury may have been included, along with some that were actually play bites, particularly since even experts do not necessarily agree on the latter distinction.

In fact, dogs aren't even the most dangerous domestic animals. That distinction surely goes to horses. With only one horse for every ten dogs in the US, equines account for one-third as many injuries as canines. Those injuries are dramatically more serious,

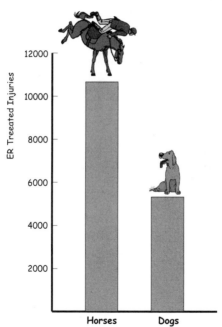

Figure 10. ER Treated Injuries to Humans
(per million animals)

For every million horses, there are over 10,000 horse-related injuries treated in emergency rooms each year. For every million dogs, only about 5,000 people are treated for dog-related injuries each year.
Data Sources: Horses—NEISS 2001–2003. Dogs—WISQAR 2001–2003.

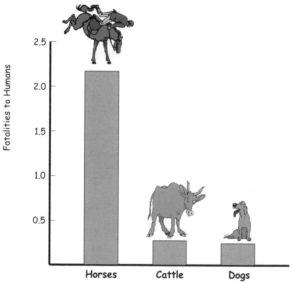

Figure 11. Fatallties to Humans (per million animals)

For every million horses, there are 2.16 human fatalities per year, making them the most dangerous domestic animals by far. There is only about one fatality per year per four million animals for both cattle and dogs, but when you consider that cattle spend much less time in contact with humans, they also loom as far more dangerous than dogs.
Data Source: US Census for fatal occupational injuries for 1992–1994.

traumatic brain injuries being foremost among them. Even cattle cause about as many injuries as dogs, though by comparison most come into contact with humans rarely and briefly.

So the reality is that dogs almost never kill people, and they don't actually bite very often, and when they do, we're seldom injured, and when we are, it's seldom serious.

So why are so many people so afraid of being bitten by a dog?

CHAPTER THREE

Fear Factors

Fear is good. It is essential to survival, perhaps even more essential than its sister, pain. Fear is the response that prompts us to take action to prevent harm to ourselves and those we care about. Fear made me slam on the brakes this morning on the way home from the dog park, when a car suddenly pulled away from the curb and sped toward my truck. Fear works most effectively when considering one's options carefully would take too much time. Fear is needed when freezing, or fleeing, or facing off the threat now will keep us alive.

But we are also a species (possibly the only one) who can think about the future, and imagine scary events there. The ability to plan is a huge evolutionary leap for our species, a major function of our rationality. Reason and fear don't talk to each other much, though. They're housed in different rooms of our brains and psyches, and often estranged.

Stone-Age Fears In The 21st Century

The scientists who developed the discipline they named risk analysis soon discovered the schism between fear and reason.

They were attempting to quantify, and thus help, people to scale the risks involved in emerging technologies like nuclear power, where the potential harmful consequences didn't lend themselves well to trial and error learning about risks. What they discovered, however, was that rationally derived information about the level of danger didn't have much effect on people's perceptions, on how afraid they actually were of a given possibility in their environment.

Turns out, the kind (rather than the immanence or magnitude) of danger we're faced with is tied to very old, very deep, self-protective impulses. So the intensity of our fear is only tenuously related, if at all, to the seriousness of the danger.

Sometimes the actions we take to avoid minor risks put us in much greater harm's way than having done nothing. In other words, we can create big problems by making major alterations in our environment in an attempt to avoid things that are extremely unlikely to occur in the first place.

What Drives The Risk Perception Thermostat?

"I didn't volunteer for this"

According to the social psychologists who have researched risk perception factors, people see a hazard that they didn't volunteer to be exposed to as representing a greater danger than one taken on willingly. So the idea of a dangerous dog conjures up the image of a marauding pack of semi-feral animals on the loose attacking strangers, even though the vast majority of bites (fatal and non fatal) are delivered to people the dogs know in the dogs' own homes.

"I can't control this"

Related to the reluctance in being drafted into a risky situation is the increased hazard perceived when people see a risk as uncontrollable. Since very few people know much about dog behavior, dog aggression usually appears to them to be unpredictable and unprovoked.

"This isn't right"

Ignorance of dog behavior opens the door to exacerbated responses to a risk when its existence is perceived to be immoral. This is one of the many harms that come from the ubiquitous error of interpreting dog behavior in ethical terms. Aside from being ridiculous, it leads to seeing the biting dog as evil by nature, as acting out of malice, and therefore, that much more frightening.

"This has never happened to me"

Then there is the familiar versus unfamiliar factor. I often think it would be helpful if everybody were to sustain a dog-bite injury to the most common level of severity, which is probably about that of a stubbed toe. Or perhaps a bit more intensely. I know I am much less afraid of being bitten by a dog than I was before I'd had the experience. The unknown sensation was much worse than the reality, which was just something (like lots of other mishaps in my life) that hurt for a while and then went away. It became a level of harm I could elect, or not elect, to put myself in the way of, rather than something to be avoided at all costs, an all or nothing position which might well turn out to be too costly.

"Everybody's talking about this"

In 2001, when the first dog-bite fatality since there have been records of such things occurred in San Francisco, the papers and

TV and radio covered little else for weeks. A quick search of the main news database yielded over 200 newspaper articles on the event in the month following, and that's just California newspapers. An equal number were spread out over the rest of that year, and the two years following yielded another 150. Grasping at straws to pass off as information (facts about the incident were very scarce), the awareness of perceived risk increased as people were deluged with lurid speculations.

Soon, people began crossing the street and shielding their children, or worse, grabbing sticks and waving them at one of my colleagues as she walked through Golden Gate Park with her gentle, rather timid (and leashed) German Shepherd. The information bath had had its effect.

The more aware we are of a risk, the more publicity it receives, and hence the more afraid we are. Perhaps this is because up until very recently in our evolutionary history we have lived in small communities of at most a few dozen to a few hundred people, with little information from beyond our group. So on an intuitive level, we process information about strangers who are depicted in detail in the media as if they were members of our own little communities.

Certainly, a danger that kills around one in a hundred people like guns or poisons or Alzheimer's is worth putting some effort into avoiding. (According to the National Center for Health Statistics percentages of deaths by cause for 2001, each of these agents accounted for roughly 1 percent of total deaths.) The difficulty is that we hear in great, personal detail about events with a lifetime risk of one in ten thousand like drowning in the bathtub or one in a hundred thousand like dying from an insect bite or even one in a million, like being eaten by a bear. Because of this exposure, we tend to perceive those events as if they were happening all over our own neighborhoods. We just don't have the mental equipment to put them into perspective. So publicity increases fear.

"Children in peril! Children in peril!"
Risks to the next generation frighten us more than risks to adults. Recent research indicates that adults are actually bitten by dogs more often than children. But children are at elevated risk for significant (meaning medically treated) injury from dog bites. One of several possible explanations is that bites to the head and upper torso are more likely to be considered serious enough to require treatment. Children, because they are small, are more likely to be bitten on the head or upper torso, whereas adults more commonly take bites to the hands, arms, and legs.

Primal Fear—Our Alligator Brains Still Work Just Fine
And there is, of course, the "dread" factor, a slightly more sophisticated version of the what's the most horrible way you can think of to die, game.

When I was in college, I once went for a walk with friends through a Eucalyptus grove behind a picturesque California mission. As I led the way along the narrow path, the leaves a step or so ahead rustled and parted and I glimpsed a fluidly moving shaft. I did not then begin to reflect upon one of my favorite poems, "A Narrow Fellow in the Grass." I did not consider the relative likelihood of the species, say garter snake versus rattler. I did not consider how best to avoid having our paths converge. I simply began to climb my friend who was walking beside me as if he had been a tree, while managing to utter the word, "snaaaaaaaake" in a long, ascending intonation. My mind was completely filled with the necessity to feel the sensation of my feet being off the ground. It would be incorrect to describe this as a thought in the usual sense.

Since the 1980's, this kind of response has been a subject of considerable research by neurobiologists studying how the brain processes and remembers fear. In 1865, though, in the poem I mentioned earlier, Emily Dickinson described it quite precisely.

> *But never met this Fellow*
> *Attended, or alone*
> *Without a tighter breathing*
> *And Zero at the Bone—*

In all probability, the visual stimulus of the snake was being processed by a small area of my brain called the amygdala, sending impulses to my adrenal medulla, telling it to secrete epinephrine (adrenaline) which stimulated my lungs to pull in more oxygen and norepinephrine to speed up my heart rate and the blood flow to my muscles. The glucose level in my blood increased, giving me a jolt of energy. All in the interest of getting those feet off the ground.

This response may have been the result of previous learning about snakes, maybe from a book or on TV. It could have also been my first encounter with one of these creatures, as there is much evidence to support the idea of prepared learning, which simply means that the brains of members of a particular species can learn very readily, almost instantly, to respond to certain very important stimuli in predictable ways.

It makes sense in evolutionary terms for people to easily learn to fear snakes and spiders and large predators like wolves, certainly, as we've spent most of our history as a species as sometime prey for larger or better armed creatures. We needed a very big fear response to get us out of those situations.

The Science Of "Yikes"

The findings of neurobiologists who have studied the physiology of fear suggest that scary experiences result in emotional memories that are directly hooked into our neurochemical and sensory systems, without mediation through the conscious, reasoning parts of the brain. These emotional memories can then be triggered by contextual cues associated with the initial event and result in a kind of reliving of the fear, or, more precisely, of the fearful event itself, without much cognitive intervention. Fear memories are devilishly difficult to defuse, once engaged. The amygdala seems to routinely trump the cortex in situations with any emergency potential.

This research (notably that of Joseph LeDoux of New York University, and beautifully explained in his book, The Emotional Brain), suggests an explanation of the risk analysts' discovery of the "dread" factor in our intuitive calculations of levels of risk. Some dangers just feel more horrible to us than others.

Clearly, for most humans, being torn to pieces by a big predator looms rather larger in our nightmares than expiring (we commonly describe it as "peacefully," although the reality often doesn't live up to this) at home in bed. Not nearly enough time has passed, evolutionarily speaking, for our brain circuitry or neurochemistry to adapt to the now much greater risks we encounter that lead to us dying in bed.

The 6 O'clock News As One More Reality Show

Barry Glassner, the noted University of Southern California professor of sociology, puts forward some additional explanations for exaggerated fears. His best selling book, The Culture of Fear, is a tour de force compilation of grotesque media-disseminated misinformation and misinterpretations of the dangers of contemporary life.

He proposes that much of this is driven by the media thirst for lurid, simplistic copy, by special interest groups with axes to grind, and by a kind of cultural scapegoating, a search for unambiguous villains that allows us to distance ourselves from responsibility for the real problems in our society. The fatal dog-bite case in January of 2001 in San Francisco had aspects of all of these.

Very Trivial Event—Film at 11!

This horrific case sensitized a whole city to images of ferocious canines, in much the way a horror movie causes you to jump out of your skin at the slightest noise for hours afterward. As a result, any dog-related incident, no matter how minor, rated TV coverage and front-page status and presumably sold papers for months. Making reference to the fatal case of Diane Whipple of the week before, reporters for the San Francisco Chronicle ran prominent stories about a woman who "knew I was going to die," when her neighbor's Cane Corso, ran across the street and bit her on the arm.

The next week, on February 5th, the Chronicle reported a "rampaging" Pit who ran around a school yard "like a mad dog," nipping several kids before being shot by police. Crisis counseling was being arranged for the "traumatized" kids.

60

A few weeks later, on March 18th, the same paper featured a story about another woman who was bitten on the arm as she tried to break up a fight between a neighbor's Pit Bull and her own Akita. The reporter admitted that the woman's wound amounted to a single "superficial laceration" (shallow cut to you and me), which was duly swabbed with antiseptic and Band-Aided at the local ER. Neither dog was seriously injured in the dog fight. A police officer arrived on the scene after the dog fight was over. He shot the Pittie 16 times because he "felt the dog was going to attack him." His colleague then shot the dead dog 14 more times.

Nutty Numbers—How 2 Becomes A Trend

These sorts of incidents continued to get press until about a month after the San Francisco fatality, when a 10-year-old boy riding his bike in Richmond, about 15 miles outside the city, was seriously bitten by two or three loose dogs and sustained critical injuries that eventually required extensive reconstructive surgery. Immediately, language like "wave of attacks" began to appear on editorial pages.

Finally, A Bite They Could Sink Their Teeth Into

It was 22 months before the local media got another serious incident to report, the case of a small boy who lost most of one ear to a loose dog in the suburbs about 30 miles outside of San Francisco. The child spent 36 hours in intensive care in a local hospital as a result, although his injuries were never critical. The stories that appeared in several local newspapers for the four days following the incident bear out another of Glassner's points, that there is less concern with facts than with titillation in this kind of reporting.

So the child was first four then three years old. He lived in Fremont, then in neighboring Milpitas. He was walking home from a park when he was bitten, or he was being carried by his aunt, or his mother. The aunt (or mother) was "attacked" by the dog, but curiously sustained no injuries even though the child was "ripped" from her arms. The owner of the dog was described variously as a relative of the boy, then as a neighbor, then as a convicted drug dealer.

If It Bit, It Must Be A Pit

The dog (named Cain or Kain) was described sometimes as a Pit Bull (that vast, vague category of dogs, about which there is no agreement as to which dogs should actually be included) or as an American Bull Terrier (which does not exist). There is a breed called a Bull Terrier (which is English in origin), and recognizable to most people as Spuds Mackenzie of beer commercial fame. There is an American Staffordshire Terrier, an American Pit Bull Terrier, a Staffordshire Terrier (a smallish, English dog) a Bulldog (the well known Winston Churchill look-alike) and an American Bulldog (Michael J. Fox played the voice of Chance, the American Bulldog, in the Disney tearjerker, Homeward Bound). There are also American Eskimo Dogs, American Foxhounds, and American Cocker Spaniels, although I suspect the reporter's priority was to get the word "bull" in the name, rather than American.

But, to me, the most fascinating bit of reporting on this incident was that of the police officer who was not there. He declared, nevertheless, in feckless defiance of the laws of geometry, not to mention canine anatomical engineering, that "the dog had the boy's head clamped in his jaws."

Isn't That A Pachyderm In Your Bedroom Slippers?
In any case, the elephant in the living room here, from the Glassner perspective, is the disproportionate coverage given to this kind of event while the kinds of injuries that far more frequently disable and kill people remain almost invisible as far the media are concerned. An average day in the US, for example, ends with 117 people dead in car accidents. Yet a news search of the day the little boy was bitten by Kain the mystery dog yields only five car accidents that actually made the news. This focus on extraordinary events makes a perfect recipe for irrational fear that can lead us to make dangerous choices. Much of that danger is to the dogs, of course, but by no means all.

And still, dogs almost never kill people, and they don't actually bite very often, and when they do, we're seldom injured, and when we are, it's seldom serious. Our irrational fears have led, probably inevitably, to equally irrational attempts to address the "dog-bite problem." Before embarking on a discussion of these attempts, however, it seems appropriate to explore some of the reasons that domestic dogs have come to exhibit such a remarkably low level of aggression toward human beings.

CHAPTER FOUR

So Why Don't Dogs Hurt People More Often?

It always comes down to economics. I used to walk my dog to a little-league field every morning. The guy who took care of the field for the town collected buckets of leftover popcorn from the movie theater and scattered it around the infield for the birds. As Willy and I came around the scorekeepers' booth behind home plate and into view from the field, the crows would begin to take off. They were all gone by the time any of the seagulls even stopped eating to look at us. The seagulls left when I opened the gate to let Willy onto the field.

The pigeons, though, kept munching even as my big Rottie-Shepherd mix dashed toward them, grabbing a last morsel before finally taking off with him only a couple of yards away. If he hadn't been with me, I doubt they would have left at all. The pigeons were able to exploit more of the popcorn resource by being less easily scared off—a smaller flight distance between them and us meant they had more time to eat.

The Evolution Of Domestication: Less Fear Equals More Food

The most current theory explaining the latest DNA evidence that dogs separated from wolves about 15,000 years ago suggests, according to a 2003 Science Magazine article, that they have a lot in common with those pigeons. The last wolves to leave the prehistoric little-league field, or more likely, the only ones to approach so close to human habitations in the first place, gradually developed into dogs. Where was the profit in this? Wherever humans congregate, there is edible refuse, garbage and poop to you and me. The wolves who were less afraid of humans could exploit this bonanza, and as probably the largest animal to do this in most cases, without too much competition. They had diversified, adding scavenging to their heretofore primary means of earning a living, predation. This is not to say the humans weren't dangerous to these less easily frightened wolves. They almost certainly were, probably chasing off the proto dogs, maybe even hitting one over the head for a meal from time to time. But all in all, the risk to rate-of-return ratio benefited the ones who didn't scare too easily, and they flourished in their new economic niche.

The Problem With Fear As A Training Tool

This is one of the many things that are wrong with training methods that advise people to control their dogs' behavior with force. The first reason that dogs are so much safer than wolves for humans to be around is that they're not afraid of us, which wolves certainly are. Any action that leads to making them afraid of us (and fear is fear, no matter what the euphemism, like "respect"), is likely to lead to biting, since predators mostly say, "yikes," with their teeth. Of course dogs do bite us. The astonishing thing is that they don't bite us more often and harder.

Raccoons Are Freeloaders Too

Dogs are certainly not the only mammalian species to have developed a symbiotic relationship with humans. In the city where I live now, the first dogs' ancient income source is mostly exploited by raccoons. I hear or see them rummaging around in my or my neighbors' backyards so often that I never let my dogs out at night without checking for the masked bandits first. And they have little enough fear of me so that it takes some doing to run them off. They don't seem to like bright lights in their eyes, and trundle off casually when I shine a flashlight at them. I've noticed that they will usually move away if I just approach, but sometimes they stand their ground and threaten, so I guess that makes me a potential predator after all, albeit an apparently not very scary one. I don't know what they'd do if I continued to press, and am not anxious to find out—hence the flashlight technique. I certainly have no inclination to try to pat one. Nor have I ever seen one make any move toward me that looked remotely like, "Hiya, wanna be friends?"

There are really only three common ways for animals to view one another across species lines: You're my lunch; I'll be your lunch if I'm not careful; and, neither of the above and therefore uninteresting. I probably drift between the last 2 categories in the raccoons' view.

From Scavenger To Companion—The Great Canine Leap

So what's even more unusual about the evolution of dogs is that they took the next step, actually interacting with humans, and thereby conferring many inadvertent, perhaps, but real benefits on us, their human companions. The most amazing aspect of our relationship with dogs is the utterly unique level of intimacy and tolerance it represents.

There is, quite simply, no other widespread interspecies relationship anything like it. Dogs not only bond with us; they do not require that we stay within the bounds of what would be acceptable behavior within the members of their parent species, wolves. We don't have to act like dogs for dogs to tolerate and even enjoy and solicit the interaction. They, however, seem to take some of the social behaviors that serve to keep the peace and facilitate bonds among themselves and apply them to their interactions with us.

Don't Try That With A Tame Wolf

This is one of the most interesting, to my mind, questions about dogs. How did they come to let, even invite, us to behave toward them in ways that would be met with swift and heavy retribution among wolves? The biologist Ray Coppinger, in his book on the evolution of dogs, writes of vigorously patting a wolf in response to the instruction to "just treat them like dogs." The wolf had been born in captivity, had been hand raised, and was handled by humans daily.

Nevertheless, when Coppinger began patting the wolf as he would a dog, he was immediately attacked by several animals, to the sound of the wolf behaviorist screaming, "Get out, get out, they'll kill you!" What Coppinger learned was that to achieve even a modicum of safety in interacting with "tame" wolves, one must enter the wolves' world, carefully observing and imitating their body language and patterns of interaction.

Of course, some actions that are taken as threatening among dogs are also seen as threats by some dogs when humans perform them. Many dogs, for example, don't like prolonged direct eye contact. Such behavior often precipitates (or at least precedes) a squabble among dogs.

Even more dogs do not like to be approached when they have valuable resources like yummy, meaty bones. And they like having those things actually taken away from them even less. Unlike wolves, these dogs can almost always be taught not to fear and thus not to react defensively to such behavior on the part of humans. Astonishingly, however, many dogs, even without specific training, accept such interactions with aplomb.

Making Dogs—The Silver Fox Experiments

How might this have come about? Perhaps the best hypotheses to date can be formulated by looking at the famous experiments of the Russian geneticist, Dmitry Balyaev, with foxes. Balyaev, and his colleagues who have continued his work since his death, have selectively bred Siberian Silver Foxes for tameness for 40 years, and they have produced something very like an extremely friendly dog. These fox-dogs eagerly approach, cuddle, and lick human faces, while competing with each other for human attention. In other words, they act much like puppies, displaying what we often label "active submission" even as they develop into adulthood. These fox-dogs look, by the way, rather like Border Collies.

The scientists accomplished this by selecting exclusively for what they called "tameability." They carefully defined, quantified, and tested for tameability (by handling the pups in structured ways at set intervals and charting their responses) and then only bred those who scored highest on this scale. This meant they started by breeding the most docile foxes, then as they had more and more of these to choose from, progressed to breeding only the most actively friendly ones.

The Development Of Fear

One major discovery in the course of this genetic manipulation was that in changing the social behavior of these foxes toward humans, they had dramatically altered their neurochemistry. First, the onset of these pups' fear response was later. This is the point in virtually all mammals' development when they begin to avoid anything new.

Wariness of the unfamiliar often must compete with a conflicting curiosity, and this same group of scientists made an interesting corollary finding when they did a parallel study with wild Norwegian rats, breeding them for tameness. After 42 generations, the rats, like the foxes, were very friendly toward humans. In field tests they also showed a dramatically greater inclination to actively explore their environment than did their more aggressive counterparts, another indication of raised fear threshold.

Novelty And The "Yikes" Response

A default avoidance response is called neophobia (fear of novelty), and is obviously a very useful trait. It's what keeps the wild adult fox from trundling up to cheerfully investigate the first bear it meets. Neophobia is a developmentally triggered response: adults have it; neonates, and often juveniles, don't. This does not mean, of course, that you can't frighten a puppy; they can quickly learn to fear things that hurt them, for example. But their immediate response to new things is approach, not avoidance.

In fact, since everything is new to the newborn, if novelty frightened them, they'd be in a constant state of stress and flight. This would result in impossibly costly wear and tear on their bodies. Babies, presumably, live in a protected environment among their family group, and the things they are exposed to during this period should become familiar and perceived as safe for the rest of their lives. Adults, on the other hand, generally live longer if they respond to unfamiliar things with caution, even suspicion.

The Chemistry Of Fear

The chemicals that trigger and maintain fear responses are called corticosteriods. The onset of the big surge in these chemicals in the tameness-selected foxes gradually moved back three or more weeks. The delayed onset of neophobia gives the tamer fox pups a bigger window of opportunity to be exposed to more things (including people), so that they won't be new when encountered after the adult caution sets in.

Domestic canine puppies enjoy a similarly extended period of routinely approaching anything new, giving their owners a golden (and finite) opportunity to socialize them to all sorts of people and situations. The result of thorough socialization is an adult dog with a "been there, done that" (instead of a "yikes") attitude to whatever he met as a puppy and discovered to be benign. This includes everything from the mail carrier to the veterinarian in her scrubs, from women wearing big hats to teenagers on skateboards, from brooms to garbage trucks, from toddlers to old people leaning on canes. And so on.

Various studies have come up with differing results regarding the timeline for the closing of the "socialization window," but all agree that socializing an adult dog to novel stimuli is a remedial effort, at best.

It should hardly need to be pointed out, anything a puppy isn't exposed to early on, he will be predisposed to flee from when he encounters it later in life. Since flight is not always an option, such exposure omissions are at the root of countless growls and snarls and snaps and bites directed at unfamiliar people.

The extended socialization window in itself might have explained the tame behavior of the little Siberian foxes. But the geneticists wanted to be sure that any differences they found were entirely hereditary, not even partially a result of learning and environment. So they were very careful to minimize the puppies' contact with humans during this impressionable period. And still, the foxes grew up to be extremely affiliative with people.

Their friendly behavior may well be related to two other differences in the brain chemistry between the tame foxes and the original semi-wild captive ones. First, although the tame foxes do develop the fear response as measured by a gradual increase in basal levels of corticosteroids, the levels of these chemicals in their brains even as adults are 75 percent lower than those in the original population. They just aren't wired to scare as easily.

The Chemistry Of Confidence

Further, the tame foxes have significantly enhanced serotonin production systems. They have higher levels of serotonin, of its key metabolite (5-oxyindolacetic acid), of the enzyme involved in the production of serotonin (tryptophan hydroxylase), and lower levels of the enzyme that removes serotonin (monoamine oxidase).

This is significant because serotonin is the basic tranquility chemical in animals, including humans. Low levels of serotonin have been linked over and over to all manner of emotional distress, from anxiety to depression to anger in people. Low serotonin has been linked to aggressive behavior in species ranging from trout to hamsters to horses, to humans (although there remains some controversy about whether this effect is due to decreased impulse control or increased hostility). It's entirely possible that in selecting animals for friendly behavior toward humans, these geneticists have developed the ultimate "don't worry, be happy" animal.

These findings are, by the way, one of the many reasons that it's worth considering psychotropic medications (ones that increase serotonin levels in the brain in various ways) in working with dogs that lack the friendliness and handleability of the tame foxes. Such neurochemical intervention can serve as an adjunct to behavior modification for dogs who spend too much of their lives in fight-or-flight responses to ordinary interactions with humans.

Some, of course, will say the Russian experiments can't really tell us how natural selection works because it's artificial selection managed by humans. Nonsense. Selection is no more artificial because it is driven by human intention. Human actions are just one more source of selective pressure, like cold weather favoring migrating animals or ones with heavy fur. This idea of "artificial" selection springs from the enormous fallacy that humans exist somehow outside of the natural order simply because we are aware of it. Selection is selection. My house does not cease to shelter me because I notice it's there.

How Confident Wolves Wound Up In The Dog-Show Ring

It's quite likely that something roughly similar to the tame fox process happened in the early development of domestic dogs. The competitive edge involved tolerating ever greater proximity to humans, and the individuals who could tolerate this had lower fear thresholds. Over many generations (certainly many more than in the Russian experiments) this resulted in gradually lower and lower fear thresholds. This alteration in brain chemistry expresses itself in wagging and squirming and whining and licking and such behaviors that humans happen to easily recognize as friendly and often find appealing. So the few individuals at the highest end of these behaviors are likely to have graduated from a dash and grab style of making a living to actually being given tidbits from time to time.

When there were too many of these friendly pups around for them to seem special, well, people just found other ways to pick favorites, maybe the one that barked first when a stranger approached the village, or the one with the curly hair or the white face. And we were off, irrevocably, on the road to the American Kennel Club and the Westminster Dog Show.

The selective breeding process that eventually ensued (almost certainly after millennia of something more like selective favoritism), has managed to maintain the greater part of this hormonally mediated temperament shift. This is the case even though no one, at present, actually systematically breeds for it, except, perhaps, by culling the occasional over-the-top aggressive (for a dog, that is) specimen. Dogs are, of course, sometimes euthanized for aggression, although not nearly so often as for other human cultural incompatibilities, like having the bad luck to be adopted by people who don't know how to housetrain them.

74

One exception would be Pit Bull Terriers who, up until very recently, were quite methodically bred for extremely low aggression to humans, since they had to be easily handleable, even when in an extreme state of agitation in the fighting ring. Try grabbing your gentle Retriever when she's caught a squirrel or is in the thick of a dog fight, and your understanding of this may well be enhanced by your need for first aid.

It's clear, though, that once humans got involved in breeding dogs systematically for all kinds of specific traits, both in appearance and particular behaviors, that the natural selection trend toward tamer and tamer animals became more erratic. This is partly because our knowledge of genetics is still pretty rudimentary in terms of which specific traits are linked genetically to which other traits.

The Problem With Beauty Contests

Balyaev's Silver Foxes provide a clear example. Remember, they were bred exclusively for a single trait, handleability (later modified to active affiliation). But physical traits came along for the ride. The tame foxes have piebald coats (large patches of white instead of pure black coats) for example, and ears that flop down like puppies' ears instead of standing up like the original adult foxes'. Some of the justification for the support for the original experiments was to create a more easily handled and therefore more easily farmed animal for the fur industry. It's quite feasible that if the scientists had insisted on retaining the pure black coats, they would have made less progress in breeding friendlier and friendlier animals.

Now people who decide to breed their dogs may have a dizzying array of traits in mind. Those who allow their intact animals to wander about and breed randomly may have nothing coherent in mind at all. The most common mode of acquiring puppies in this country, however, is through breeders of pedigreed dogs. Pedigreed dogs are bred, overwhelmingly, for their looks, the measure of success in the dog-show ring. Thus a large percentage of breedings have as their object the appearance of the dogs. Cuteness, conformation, and coat color are the driving forces behind show breeding decisions, however much these qualities may depend upon the eye of the beholder.

Among breeders, any effect of, say, the number and pattern of spots on a Dalmatian, or the length and silkiness of the hair on an Afghan, or the size of the head on a Bulldog on the animal's temperament is a remotely distant second in importance to the physical trait itself. It's pure chance whether or not the physical traits selected for will carry any desirable behavior traits with them.

Many breeders claim, of course, to "breed for temperament," but I've yet to meet one who declined to breed a really successful show dog (or even one the breeder thought could contribute to her future success in the breed ring) because it was aggressive, unless it was so uncontrollable that it couldn't be trained or at least managed well enough to, say, not bite the judge.

Forgetting The Marquis Of Queensberry Rules
Still, dogs that actually injure people are pretty routinely culled in most circles, so the general adaptive trend over the millennia has continued to favor animals that are not seriously aggressive. There are, of course, exceptions.

It is fashionable to blame certain segments of society for deliberately breeding dangerous dogs. I wonder if there is much of this really going on, however. As mentioned before, dogs systematically bred for dog fighting are unlikely to present much of a threat to humans. For one thing, the traits selected for in fighting dogs are probably not even related to those that increase the likelihood of common forms of dog aggression toward humans. To get dogs that engage in long duration, sometimes even fatal fights with other dogs, you must first select for animals with high pain thresholds. While such a dog may be more difficult to train using pain, or more precisely avoiding pain, as a motivator, this in no way increases the likelihood that he will bite you.

You must also select out the species-wide tendency to stop fighting when the other animal signals one of several wolf and dog ways of saying "uncle." Responding to these cutoff signals goes back much farther than even the earliest proposed domestication timelines, since it's crucial to the ability of well armed, but social animals to settle disputes without unnecessarily diminishing their own numbers. This response is the reason why dog scraps, especially those involving only two animals, are usually quickly resolved.

Human beings, however, are extremely unlikely to do things like freeze, or roll on our backs to expose our groins, or lick our lips and turn our heads away while being bitten or even threatened by a dog. So the relative lack of aptitude for reading these signals among fighting breeds is pretty much irrelevant to dog-human aggression. The genetic origin of this basic social communication is so deep that the tendency is for it to pop back up anyway. It must be constantly, meticulously selected out of fighting stock. In any case, however widespread the practice of dog fighting may be, systematic breeding for this purpose cannot possibly account for the obvious population explosion among the so called fighting breeds.

Mr. Universe, Not Mike Tyson

Most of these dogs are clearly being bred for appearance as much as any show dog, albeit for physical traits that many humans find intimidating, like large size, heavily muscled, short-backed, wide-chested builds, and big heads with relatively short muzzles which translate into widely gaping mouths. These seem smiley to me, but clearly are perceived otherwise by many people. We choose our dogs, much as we choose our lovers, mostly by how they look—conformation, cuteness, and coat color.

Predation Specialists

It has not always been so. Many breeds of dogs were originally developed to emphasize specific behavioral tendencies that made them useful as work animals. Some skewed behavior toward compulsive predation, without completing the sequence through the kill, like livestock-herding dogs and retrievers. So you get dogs like the beloved Golden Retriever of my childhood, Tracy, who worked for hours figuring out how to get the parakeet's cage door open, then proudly trotted up and placed the bird, completely unharmed, into my grandmother's hand. She had never had a single retrieve-training session.

This kind of single-trait selection explains why I had to monitor frisbee throwing into the lake among groups of students I used to take on picnics. Oliver, my amiable, 110-pound Newfoundland/Golden Retriever cross, would continue to swim after the frisbee past the point where he was gasping and staggering out of the water, half-drowned from exhaustion. It also explains the circular dirt track my parents' Cattle Dog wore into the lawn, as she spent hours every day trying to herd the Mulberry tree.

Breeding For Yikes—Professional Neophobics

Rather more ominous are those breeds that were selected to protect livestock or people from intruders. The breed standards for these dogs, categorized mainly as flock guardians and protection dogs, often use euphemisms like "reserved" and "intensely loyal to their owners" to describe their breed's attitude toward people. Unpack this, and what you're really selecting for is heightened neophobia: a bite first, ask questions later approach to anything or anyone unfamiliar. This is, as should be obvious by now, exactly the opposite of traits that are likely to result in amiable, affiliative animals suitable as household companions. And yet, perversely, people often want both of these almost certainly mutually exclusive packages of traits in the same animal.

White Hats/Black Hats—It's All The Same To Dogs

The fantasy is the dog who will identify and attack the bad guy while remaining docile and affectionate with all well intentioned people. And so people often cite "protection" as one reason for acquiring a family pet. We must let this go. Suspicion of unfamiliar people is a generalized trait, not a specific one. So the dog that is likely to bite a burglar is even more likely to bite Great-Aunt Suzie when she comes tottering in, leaning on her walker.

While it is possible to train dogs to attack people on cue or in response to specific behaviors, this is an extremely technically challenging task. It requires the most advanced, and most likely to wobble, level of training—stimulus control. Stimulus control means that the animal never offers the behavior without the cue. It is never completely fail safe.

79

DOGS BITE: BUT BALLOONS AND SLIPPERS ARE MORE DANGEROUS

Because the protection myth is still so prevalent, there are people hyping various designer breeds, like the Caucasian Mountain Dog, a huge, fluffy, teddy-bear-looking Russian-derived flock guardian.

A Web site dedicated to promoting this 180-pound dog enthuses that it is "the answer to crime in America," but advises caution lest it "be aggressive towards an unannounced visitor or the UPS delivery person carrying that strange-looking package which could be a threat to the family." The writer further sings the Caucasian's praises as "unsurpassed in the U.S. today in providing serious protection for the home and family."

As long as it is acceptable to actually promote a dog as "territorial and suspicious of strangers," and to selectively breed pet animals that "will protect their flock, family, and property from danger real or perceived with lightening-quick speed," we will continue to have some dogs on the dangerous end of the aggression continuum. It is this profound ambivalence about what we really want from dogs that is a huge factor at the root of any problems that actually exist in terms of aggression of dogs toward humans.

CHAPTER FIVE

The Bird and the Bird Dog: Or, What Is Aggression, Anyway?

Most mornings I awaken to a deep rumbling sound, followed by a sharp clack. If I look in the direction of the pillow next to mine, I am greeted by the sight of my red Doberman, Ruby, lips flexed to show her bright pointed teeth, darting her muzzle toward me as she snaps her jaws together. What are we to infer from this?

The Traumatized Retriever

You may remember Chipper the parakeet from an earlier chapter when he was plucked from his cage and presented to my grandmother by Tracy, the lovely Golden Retriever who was my first dog. What I didn't mention was that my grandmother then hit Tracy on the head, hard enough to bounce the dog's jaws together and break off Chipper's tail. And poor Tracy was so impressed by this single instance of punishment that she never attempted to retrieve anything again. She did, however, growl once when I approached her too closely while she was busy eating her breakfast. When I complained tearfully to my mother of this awful betrayal, that sometimes sensible woman replied brusquely, "What's the matter with you? What are you doing bothering the dog when she's eating?"

Now Tracy was not, in point of absolute fact, my first dog. Shortly before I acquired Chipper, the neighbors' Sheltie cross had had an impromptu litter and one of the pups had been presented to me by said neighbors as a well meant, if ill-considered, Christmas gift. My little brother was not quite walking at the time, and the new puppy repeatedly jumped on him as he sat unsteadily in the backyard, knocking him down, much to my mother's consternation. The puppy was duly relegated to the pound, and the resulting trauma led me inevitably down the road to becoming a professional dog trainer, thus continuing my mother's dismay arising from this incident into much later life.

Chipper's Saga

But let's return to Chipper, who had the misfortune to be my first pet, with the exception of the unlucky Tippy. When he came into my life, I was eager to teach him to perch on my hand. The first time I attempted this, he immediately grabbed onto my finger with surprising, and quite painful, force. I reacted instantly with my seven-year-old lack of impulse control by shaking my finger as hard as I could to dislodge him. The resulting centrifugal force eventually worked, pulling Chipper and a small bit of flesh off of my finger and landing him, horrifically, in a sink full of scalding dishwater. Amazingly, after his feathers grew back, he did eventually learn to ride around on my hand and shoulder.

These were not the only harrowing episodes in his life. I arrived home from school one day several years later to find my little brother and a couple of his preschool friends huddled over something under the plum tree in the front yard.

"Birdie won't fly," he complained to me when I discovered that Chipper, who was indeed flopping around ineffectually on the ground, was the object of their scrutiny.

The little boys had been examining the poor bird in an attempt to solve the mechanical mystery of flight and had, in the process, managed to dislocate both of Chipper's wings. It wasn't too long after he got his splints off that he took advantage of a door carelessly left open and flew away. Who can blame him?

Everyday Conflicts, Threats, And Force

I'm subjecting you to all these gloomy, sometimes violent, tales because it seems to me that if we are going to talk intelligibly about the phenomenon of biting dogs, we need to establish some idea of what we mean when we speak of aggression generally. The word is thrown around willy-nilly in the legal and popular literature on the subject of dangerous dogs, to such an extreme that it is frequently used interchangeably with vicious, a term with connotations of depravity and malice that are simply absurd when applied to dogs. We have absolutely no access to the dog's intention regarding his opponent, if, indeed, he has any. Yet the implication in discussions of growling or snarling or biting is usually that an aggressive dog is "bad," in the moral sense.

If we can find a way to decide what we mean by aggression, we still need to determine whether there is an identifiable line between appropriate and inappropriate demonstrations of aggression in the world of a domestic animal. Ideally, this would be some watershed that helps us predict which animals present an elevated risk of injury to people.

First things first. Let's compile the actions in the preceding domestic dramas and see whether we can determine which are examples of aggression. Here's what we have:

- Dog snapping and/or growling at a human when it's time to get up in the morning
- Dog catching parakeet in jaws and presenting to a human
- Human hitting dog on head to get dog to drop bird
- Puppy knocking down toddler
- Woman surrendering puppy to dog pound
- Parakeet grabbing onto human finger placed within reach
- Child flinging parakeet into sink
- Children dislocating parakeet's wings during examination
- Dog growling when approached while eating

Much of the confusion about aggressive behavior in animals may spring from confounding the language used in the sciences of animal behavior with everyday language meanings. A decent dictionary will tell you that when people say "aggressive" in ordinary conversation, they usually mean something like "an unprovoked attack, or act of hostility," with hostility, in turn, referring to an "emotional state of enmity" or "general feeling of antagonism."

And more recently, aggression has come to designate any pushy behavior among humans. The word always carries a pejorative connotation, except, oddly, when applied to men (but not women) in professional situations, as in "he aggressively sought out new clients," where it seems to mean energetic pursuit of a goal.

Provocation Is A Useless Concept Here

When referring to dog behavior, definitions such as those discussed above clearly will not do. First of all, the whole concept of provocation with regard to animals is a hopeless quagmire. If we mean by provocation the common implication that the victim deserved it, that the attacker was justified, we're placed in the untenable position of deciding who's morally in the right in an interspecies dispute, when humans are the only species that can be demonstrated to construct ethical concepts in the first place.

By justifiable, we usually mean situations where we can imagine ourselves lashing out. According to this kind of interpretation, if you decide that Chipper did not do anything to deserve having his wings pulled half off, my little brother's curious examination was clearly aggressive, while Tracy's growling over her food bowl was not, at least according to my mother.

If, on the other hand, we use the more literal, non-connotative meaning of provocation as simply that which elicits action, then all threats and attacks are by definition provoked. Moreover, we have no access to the dog's internal emotional state, so the whole question of hostility, much less what actions on the part of other organisms might provoke it, is unusable as part of our definition.

We do have some information on neurochemical changes that occur in some situations in both humans and other animals where the human emotional states are known (or at least reported by the subjects since we can never know for certain what another human is experiencing). We can thus hypothesize that the non-humans are experiencing similar feelings. But this is by no means a settled question, and in any case, the existing neurochemical research on emotion does not cover anything like the breadth of situations that we refer to as aggressive.

Science Has Its Own Dictionaries

And yet, I would submit that it is possible to formulate a reasonable definition of aggression and that most, but not all, of these acts would qualify. The answer lies in scientific definitions of aggression, those that have been offered by ethologists and biologists who study behavior. These are the scientists who study animal behavior by watching them, alone and groups, in captive and free settings, and tabulating their actions in various situations. A famous example was Konrad Lorenz, whose discovery that goslings would resolutely follow the first creature they saw as hatchlings was used to such dramatic effect by the makers of the remarkable movie, Winged Migration.

While there is no single agreed-upon meaning of the term among scientists, commonly offered definitions of aggression include "a physical act or threat of action by one individual that reduces the freedom or genetic fitness of another" (Wilson 1975), and "actions [that] cause or threaten to cause injury to another individual" (Leshner 1978). Genetic fitness refers to the capacity of any living being to pass on its genetic material (copies of its genes) to the next generation.

Few of us would grant, though, that all actions that injure are aggressive. As a teenager, for example, I sustained various injuries (including sprains, lacerations, many contusions and one broken bone) as a direct result of horses coming to abrupt halts in front of hurdles, or leaping suddenly sideways to avoid some real or phantom danger. These actions on the part of the horses, however, had nothing to do with me; I was just along for the ride, or abrupt end thereof.

We can probably agree that we do not mean to include such accidentally harmful outcomes in the same category as the nasty, baseball-sized bite I sustained when I foolishly turned my back on my uncle's pastured Quarter Horse stud. But we're still left with the problem of the unknowability of the intent of another creature, especially one of a different species.

There is a way out of this difficulty. Scientific analyses of behavior presume adaptive significance, that is, that in order to be passed on from one member of the species to another, a behavior usually increases the likelihood of an animal surviving and having opportunities to reproduce, thereby passing on its genes. Thus we can amend one of our definitions to make explicit the assumed adaptive significance. The new definition would be something like, "a physical act or threat of action by one individual that reduces the freedom or genetic fitness of another, and increases the genetic fitness of the aggressor."

Let's look at some of our examples to see how closely they fit this definition.

Tracy vs. Chipper
Tracy grabbing poor Chipper seems to qualify quite easily. A dog catches a bird: the bird loses both freedom and fitness, and the dog

gains fitness, in the form of lunch. The fact that she didn't eat the parakeet, instead presenting it to a person, is simply a predatory misfire, selectively bred into dogs by humans wanting bird-hunting assistants. The impulse to chase and catch small, fast-moving creatures is pure predatory aggression.

While all behaviorists classify this as a category of aggression, it is important to note that predation is biologically profoundly different from all the other types of aggression we will discuss. The neurochemical processes going on when a dog is chasing and catching a rabbit are quite distinct from those that occur when the same animal is chasing away an intruder on his territory, or threatening or biting someone who tries to take a bone away from him, or defending himself from an attack like being suddenly grabbed by the collar. This last accounted for fully 20 percent of the bite cases in Dr. Ian Dunbar's large aggression practice over a period of several years. In all these situations the areas of the brain involved are those associated with fear: in a nutshell, the animal is upset. In the case of predation, he is not.

So in categorizing aggression, the biggest distinction is between predatory aggression and everything else. From the dog's perspective, predation does not involve conflict, although the rabbit, of course, would not agree. Predation (except when frustrated) does not involve threats or displays—the last thing the hunter needs to do is telegraph his intention to his prey. Nor is it likely to involve hostility. Tracy probably didn't hate Chipper, any more than you hated the cow that went into the Big Mac you ate yesterday. She was just having fun.

Verdict: predatory aggression

Grandma vs. Tracy

Grandma hitting Tracy to get her to release the bird is slightly more complicated. Tracy's freedom to retain the bird was certainly reduced, as was her genetic fitness, as she'd been punished for a basic food-getting behavior and was thus less likely to engage in it again. In fact she was so quashed by the experience that she never chased a small, fast moving creature or object again.

In Grandma's case, we have to speculate about motivation, but when you consider that she had spent most of her life on a farm and that the worst transgression a farm dog can commit is to kill or even pester livestock (most commonly chickens), it is very likely that she was responding to an impulse to prevent another predator from competing for food belonging to humans. This is at the core of most of what is classified as competitive (or sometimes "dominance") aggression—strong messages to "get away from my stuff." I do not, by the way, mean to imply that Grandma was in the habit of preparing parakeet stew, simply that seeing a dog with an owned animal in its mouth was a stimulus that caused her to immediately and directly intervene.

Verdict: competitive aggression

Tracy vs. Janis

Grandma's blow to Tracy's head was pretty much the same kind of "get away from my stuff" action as Tracy's growl at me over her food bowl. The difference was that Grandma used actual force while Tracy just threatened. When I think of the role of threats in aggression, I always think of Danny Glover in Silverado. He is standing on a cliff above some bad guys who are about to kill his friend. He cocks his rifle and says, "I don't want to kill you, and you don't want to be dead." The villains are, unsurprisingly, dissuaded from their nefarious intention.

The vast majority of competitive confrontations among members of species who rely on social bonds to increase their chances of survival are resolved without actual force. Tracy's growl at me over the food bowl is an example. The "stuff," by the way, that potential competitors may be warned away from doesn't have to be food. It can just as easily be toys (meaning any object one values) or comfy sleeping spots, one's general territory, or even people whose attention one want to monopolize, especially potential sexual partners.

Verdict: competitive aggression

The Last Meaty Bone On Earth

Humans (along with other primates) and dogs are very similar in this respect. Think of how you feel when someone, uninvited, reaches across the restaurant table and scoops the last bite of guacamole off your plate with the last tortilla chip. You probably don't actually stab them with your fork, but this is largely because you understand that you can afford the loss—it's not the last food you'll ever see.

This is usually also true for pet dogs, but they have no access to the information. So while the pet dog's response of defending his stuff in a context of plenty has been aptly described by Dr. Ian Dunbar as "paranoid," dogs have no way to know that it is unnecessary, unless we actively train them to welcome our intrusion. Of course, it is quite easy to prevent this "paranoia" in young dogs by repeatedly approaching them and tossing fabulous treats whenever they are in possession of something good. See Jean Donaldson's book, *Mine,* for ways to work with dogs who are already uncomfortable with such approaches.

Dogs' entire evolutionary history (with the exception of very recent cohabitation with humans in a few affluent cultures) has taken place in a context of scarcity; there is seldom enough to go around. In a dog's ancestral world, he who eats last often doesn't eat at all. Scarcity is all they know.

Of course there are exceptions made between particular individuals or in particular contexts. When Ruby first came into the household, Willy routinely brought her treasures, or immediately abandoned his when she approached. This changed over time, though, in what is ever-so-tempting to view as the end of the honeymoon (or courtship). Who knows. Gradually, Willy began going about the house, collecting all the dog toys, rawhides and bones, maybe eight or ten at any given time, placing them carefully in front of himself and lying down to survey his collection. Ruby would lurk a few feet away, looking at his riches with pathetic longing, as she had learned he would not let her approach and take one. He did continue, on occasion, to casually abandon his stash after a time, which meant it was safe for her to take them.

Dog toys, by the way, are generally very prey-like; they are things appropriate for chasing and gnawing and dissecting, and as such are very closely associated with food-getting behaviors. The point is that the default response among social animals is to keep what they've got, by force if it's necessary. It usually isn't.

"I Don't Want To Kill You, And You Don't Want To Be Dead."
Force directed at members of his own group is just too expensive for an animal whose chances of surviving and reproducing are enhanced by living and hunting with others. He can't afford to be

constantly thinning the ranks by maiming or killing his companions. So social species, especially those with formidable defensive and predatory weapons, develop elaborate "back off or else" signals. And most dogs listen to these signals most of the time just as most humans listen to such signals from other humans. Among both species, vocal and posturing conflicts are much more common than actual scraps.

Even when there are scuffles between dogs, in the vast majority of cases, these are quickly resolved, and the dogs "pull their punches" in the sense that they either don't make actual contact at all or inhibit the pressure of their jaws so that no one is injured. A recent study of dogs at a busy Indianapolis dog park serves as an illustration. The researchers observed a total of 177 dogs during peak dog-park attendance hours over a period of eight months. Now one could expect a dog park, with its constantly changing population to be the site of frequent battles. Dogs, like most animals, and wolves certainly among them, generally meet strangers of their own species with hostility.

Yet the researchers saw only 14 full-contact scuffles, none lasting more than 60 seconds. They observed 14 more encounters that may have been fights, but could not definitely be distinguished from rough play. There were no serious injuries at all. Even taking into consideration that a dog-park population is probably somewhat more amiable than a random population, as at least some people who know their dogs tend to get in fights will avoid dog parks, this is a remarkably low incidence of physical conflict.

Given the unprecedented interspecies intimacy between dogs and people, it is completely unsurprising that competitive aggression pops up between us. In fact, dogs are rather more likely to let us have free access to their food than we are to give them free access to ours.

Having evolved as creatures who oscillated between gorging and fasting, many canines would continue to eat everything available until they were physically unable to continue. Most people don't want their dogs eating the best, most expensive food in the house. So we prevent them from eating us out of house and home. We put the stuff we don't want them to eat where they can't get it.

And some of them, some of the time, attempt to directly prevent us from taking or threatening to take their stuff. So Tracy growled over her food bowl, and Grandma hit Tracy when she took something belonging to people.

Tippy Vs. Baby Brother

Now, how about Tippy (the Sheltie cross puppy) jumping on my baby brother and toppling him over? The baby's freedom (to sit up unmolested presumably) was certainly reduced, and although he was uninjured in these incidents, this was pretty much by chance. He unquestionably cried as if he were mortally wounded. But did these effects on the baby benefit the puppy?

You have to know a little bit about canine behavior to answer this. Dogs and wolves jump up on each other exclusively in greeting and play contexts. This is a social bonding behavior. Harming the jumpee is of no benefit whatever to the jumper. Jumping up is never a prelude to or part of predation. Saying "Get away!" or more elegantly, increasing social distance is the adaptive function of virtually all non-predatory aggression, according to one very well respected animal behavior authority, Roger Abrantes. Jumping up has no such function. Quite the opposite.

Jumping up among dogs is an attempt to get closer, usually to the face, often for licking purposes. So while it carried considerable potential for harm to the child, Tippy's behavior can't be classified as aggressive.
Verdict: no aggression

Mother vs. Tippy

Mother taking the puppy to the pound, on the other hand, satisfies all our criteria. It reduced Tippy's freedom and fitness, probably in the most final way, as this was back in the day when most shelters killed all puppies as a matter of policy. And it increased Mom's genetic fitness by protecting her offspring, a clear example of maternal aggression, one of the categories most often cited by ethologists. And one, interestingly, that some civil codes enumerate specifically as a free pass for a dog. In such codes, when a bitch with suckling pups bites someone who gets too close, the owner is specifically exempted from liability, probably because we intuitively see such aggression as provoked.

We could, I suppose, add an additional caveat, that we only want to include actions that occur immediately in the heat of the moment, unmediated by considered intention. However, this would force us to eliminate a huge amount of what we generally consider aggressive behavior in humans and specifically to label premeditated and delegated acts of violence as non-aggression. No, I'm afraid we must consider Mother to have acted aggressively.
Verdict: maternal aggression

94

Chipper vs. Janis

In an effort, I suspect, to comfort me for the loss of the puppy, Chipper, the parakeet, was purchased at a pet store. His price couldn't possibly have supported the labor cost of careful hand-raising and taming, so when he saw a claw-like object about the size of his entire body (my hand) coming at him, it was probably for the first time. (It's useful to remember that to an undersocialized dog, much of what he encounters in the world is like that giant hand was to my poor parakeet.) Now Chipper's retreat options were pretty limited. His cage comprised an area of maybe two or three cubic feet, all of which my hand could easily reach. He did the obvious thing. He tried to defend himself with the best weapon at his disposal—his beak.

In fact, defensive aggression is another major category cited by ethologists and behaviorists, a way to say "Get away from me," most often employed when running away isn't an option. In this case, it involved reducing my freedom to attack the parakeet with my hand by reducing my fitness to do anything other than stop the pain in my finger. If you cause an attacker enough pain, she will sometimes go away.

Now in the evolutionary arms race that is predator versus prey, many predators have developed a mechanism to at least partially shut down the pain and fear systems of the brain (discussed in Chapter Four) when in the heat of the chase. In order to get most predators to back off, you have to hurt them a lot. This may have had something to do with Chipper hanging on to my finger, even as I withdrew.

Verdict: defensive aggression

Janis vs. Chipper

In any case, his defense worked, sort of. I immediately withdrew my hand from the cage, but unfortunately for both of us, Chipper was still hanging on. What I did next is open to at least two interpretations. It may be that I switched into defensive mode or perhaps simply that pain elicited aggression in myself such that I entered into "Get off me" mode, or it may be that I was randomly thrashing in an attempt to dislodge my attacker and get away.

Thrashing is a strategy so often used when animals find themselves in the role of prey, by the way, that many predators, dogs among them, have evolved to be stimulated to intensifying or even initiating predatory behavior toward things that are floundering around. At any rate, Chipper's fitness was quite dramatically reduced by landing in the sink. If left to his own devices, he certainly wouldn't have survived the recovery time needed to grow new feathers, weeks and weeks without the equipment needed to fly and earn a living or avoid predators.

Verdict—defensive or pain elicited aggression

One might argue that the scalding water was no part of anybody's plan, but the risk from any kind of hazard in the environment is automatically elevated for both combatants in the heat of any dispute. It's always a gamble to focus all one's attention on a single danger. It's the nervous system's equivalent to Butch and Sundance jumping off the cliff—there's no sense worrying about drowning when the fall will probably kill you, and both are trumped by the pursuing posse, but this doesn't nullify the former hazards.

96

Aggression And Learning

A dog trainer once remarked to me (in that "you know what I mean" tone) that we've all seen dogs who after they've bitten once, "get better at it." I mulled this over for a long time as I did not, in fact, know what she had in mind. It sounded as if she had the idea that dogs must learn how to bite, that it's a skill, like learning how to dive into a swimming pool without making a belly flop. I can remember trying to hold all that stuff in my brain as a kid—head down between arms, arms straight, bend from the waist, keep bending, keep bending, and as you fall, don't straighten up or raise your head. You try this many times and bit by bit, put it all together.

It is fantastically unlikely that biting is anything like this. It certainly isn't when children do it. However, what this trainer may have observed that led her to this idea was an increase in the frequency and perhaps even intensity of biting in situations where biting had worked for the dog, worked in the sense of getting someone or something unpleasant or scary to go away. In other words, biting is reinforceable, as is any behavior, including other behaviors that are often associated with aggression like freezing and glaring, growling, snarling, and snapping.

When any behavior is immediately followed by a pleasant stimulus (or the removal of an unpleasant one) that behavior increases in frequency. The behavior has been reinforced and the probability that the animal will soon do it again, especially in a similar situation, increases. Some theorists create a separate category for this that they call instrumental (meaning learned) aggression. In all probability, though, this is a redundant category that overlaps all our types of aggression, since any time barking or lunging, say, succeeds in increasing social distance between the dog and the scary mailman, that dog is more likely to try that same strategy next time he hears the mail slot open.

Ruby vs. Janis

But what about Ruby's morning growling and snapping, an instrumental behavior if ever there was one? I definitely taught her to do this, in the sense of increasing the probability of the behavior. Ruby is what dog trainers call a "soft" dog. This means she is easily daunted by any rough treatment. She is also extremely affiliative; she just never met a person she didn't love. So the first time she clacked her teeth together, rather like a crocodile, I was not alarmed. In fact I laughed. This happened during a training session, and as far as I can tell—I'm definitely speculating here—she did this out of frustration when I changed the rules on what would earn her a treat. I should note here, by the way, that this teeth-clacking behavior has been observed in dogs soliciting play and in courtship, so this is yet another example of the futility of trying to make definitive analyses of dogs' motives.

Leave Me Alone. I'm Having A Bad Day

Frustration aggression—sometimes called irritable aggression when it is elicited by a randomly or continuously repeated aversive stimulus, like electric shock—is yet another category often presented in the scientific literature. Irritable aggression is what makes you more likely to curse at someone who cuts you off in traffic on a day when your bad knee is acting up or when it's taken 10 attempts to get your car started.

Regardless of how Ruby's teeth-clacking started, I quickly transformed it into something else, since I found her crocodile clack so amusing that I began to give her treats whenever she did it. So of course she did it more and more. I began to refine the behavior, only rewarding those clacks that were accompanied by some lip retraction exposing her teeth, until I got a behavior I could cue with the word, "Smile." So in addition to teaching Ruby an amusing trick, I increased the likelihood of this behavior in general, particularly since I didn't have the self-discipline to completely stop rewarding the smiles I hadn't cued.

Now Ruby has always tried to get me to get up in the morning when she's ready to begin her day, meaning ready to go outside, ready for breakfast, ready to go to the dog park, etc. Her main tactics, pawing and nudging, didn't work very often. So the scene was set for her to try other behaviors that had worked for her in the past—ones with reinforcement histories, even in other contexts. I don't know how many she tried, but it was the clacks that made me laugh (instead of pulling the covers over my head or banishing her from the room). And it sometimes took several clacks to get me to begin talking to her and scratching her tummy (both reliable predictors that I'm going to actually get up), thereby reinforcing her for persisting in the behavior.

It's pretty tough to make this fit our definition of aggression. First of all, the reward for aggressive behavior is usually that the threatening something goes away. In this case, the rewards, as far as I can tell, are social interaction and breakfast. It does not escalate into a more intense version of threat or actual violence if the clack and rumbling growl don't work. It escalates into licking my ears. The only freedom I lose is the freedom to sleep late. So what we have is a case of a behavior that usually carries an aggressive purpose being used for something else altogether.

It's not always easy to identify whether a given behavior belongs in the aggression column at all, much less whether it's likely to lead to biting.

Verdict—no aggression

Some Scientists Define Life As One Long Bout Of Self Defense
If nothing else is demonstrated by these examples, at least they bring to light the absurdity of the usual connotation that aggression is bad, that we need to get rid of it, and the inference that an animal displaying this trait is somehow defective. Aggression is ubiquitous. Everybody does it. This is why "evidence of prior aggressive behavior," a criterion often used to determine legal liability or in labeling dogs legally "dangerous," is useless. So far we have no way to predict which dogs will injure people if they haven't already.

Our only good predictor of future injurious biting is prior injurious biting. Growling, snarling, and snapping tell us almost nothing about the future probability of actually hurting people. Moreover, the only good predictor of not hurting people in the future is having bitten without injuring in the past.

Aggression and violence are not identical. Violence is the application of physical force. Aggression is a much broader term, including everything from subtle warnings through lethal force. Some nonviolent aggressive behaviors, like raised voices and growls, are sometimes precursors to violent ones, but by no means always. And violent acts can certainly occur without any warnings whatsoever.

It's intuitive to assume that dogs that exhibit low (non-injurious) levels of aggression, are likely to escalate to more intense levels of

100

aggression. There is some evidence for this, but not nearly as much as one might expect. In other words, in the histories of dogs that bite, there is only a slightly higher occurrence of nonviolent aggression (barking, growling, snarling, snapping, etc.) than among dogs who don't bite. But some biting dogs don't bark, growl, bark, snarl, or snap beforehand. More important, the vast majority of aggressive dogs don't bite. And most important of all—this cannot be emphasized enough—the vast majority of biting dogs don't injure anyone. Most bites don't even qualify as force as they involve neither pain nor restraint. Their efficacy is as threat gestures, like yelling and shoving matches between humans.

To put it simply, most dogs are aggressive, as are most humans, most cats, most hamsters, most birds, etc. Aggression is the norm, not the aberration. However, dogs seldom take their aggressive actions to the point of hurting us or each other.

Lots Of Growling And Snarling And Snapping, Not Much Biting

One of the few well designed studies on threats and bites among dogs is a survey of dog-owner clients of 20 veterinary clinics in Canada. The study, led by Dr. Norma Guy of Atlantic Veterinary College, found that over 41 percent of the 3,226 dogs studied exhibited obvious aggressive behaviors toward humans (growling or snapping), but only 15.6 percent ever actually bit anyone. Even this 15.6 percent is too high, as further questioning of the owners revealed that "many of the dogs who were classified as biters . . . had only engaged in harmless mouthing" (Guy, 2001)

The total segment of the dog population that growls or snarls or snaps is almost certainly higher than Guy's 41 percent. The

Canadian study was limited to aggression toward members of the dogs' households and people the dogs knew well. The consensus among researchers (those who did this study, included) is that, while there is some overlap, the population of dogs that threaten or bite familiar people is different from those that threaten or bite strangers.

The kinds of aggression involved are profoundly different. Aggression toward familiar people is most commonly of the "Get away from my stuff," or "Don't touch me there," or "don't restrain me," variety. Aggression toward strangers is most commonly an expression of neophobia, exacerbated by being approached or even chased by the unfamiliar and therefore scary person. Behavior counselor caseloads only occasionally show the same individuals presented for both.

Including dogs that growl and snarl at strangers might actually push the overall aggression percentages up considerably. Another study of 2,000 owned dogs in the North Atlantic states of the US looked for behavior clusters (or factors) in companion dogs. This means they tried to identify behaviors that occurred in clusters in the same dog. So they found that dogs characterized by their owners as "fussy" or "picky" eaters were also ones who were likely to leave their food when alone, and unlikely to gulp or eat quickly. This becomes the behavior factor, "eating sensitivity."

The behaviorists who conducted this study, Peter Borchelt and Linda Goodloe, found only a very weak correlation between the two types of aggression toward humans they studied: aggression to family members and aggression to strangers. There was overlap between the two groups, but it was slight. The dogs who growl or snarl at or bite people they know are not much more likely to growl or snarl at or bite strangers than the dogs who display no aggression toward anybody. And the dogs who don't like strangers are not much more likely to growl at or bite their own people than the ones who threaten nobody.

This is consistent with the research on aggression across various species over the last four or five decades. What's been found is that the rate and intensity of the various kinds of aggression, e.g., defensive, irritable, competitive, predatory, etc., are influenced by different neurochemical, social, environmental, and contextual factors. Things that decrease one kind of aggression often have no effect on another or may even increase it. So it's safe to assume that the total percentage of dogs that growl or snarl or snap at a human at some time during their lives is higher than Guy and Luescher's 41 percent.

Pushing The Envelope—Aggression In The Laboratory

Aggression is a fairly widely studied phenomenon across various species, including humans, although little research has been done specifically with dogs. The aggression modalities most frequently studied are territorial (attacking unfamiliar intruders), fights between males (mainly over access to females) and predatory aggression. This is of interest to scientists primarily because aggression is so pervasive among humans. Fights between males, by the way, are by far the most frequent aggressive displays among humans across virtually all cultures, at least as reflected in the ultimate aggressive encounter, homicide (Daly and Wilson, 1988).

Topping Out—Super-Cranky Fish

The experimenter studying aggression rates in non-human species manipulates various conditions (genetic, physiological, or contextual) and then looks for differences in the rate and intensity of attacks. In one well known experiment, Stickleback fish were selectively bred for both increased and decreased aggression. The biologist, Theo Bakker, was able to lower the rate of aggressive behaviors, but was unsuccessful in trying to increase it (at least in males). In other words, it turned out that natural selection had already pushed male Sticklebacks about as far up the aggression scale as it could. The only room for manipulation was at the other end of the continuum, selecting for less aggression. What this means is that Bakker was unable to push up the average level of aggression among his breeding population. It does not mean that all the individuals were identically belligerent.

To understand this we can reflect back a bit on the Silver Fox selection experiment. You will recall that what the scientists did was to breed only the foxes who met the current criteria for affiliation toward and handleability by human strangers or near strangers, and that the occurrence of friendly behaviors in their breeding population gradually increased. This does not mean, however, that their animals stopped producing less friendly or even downright unfriendly individuals, but they produced fewer, and those pups were not bred.

At some point, in any breeding protocol, you will reach a limit, a point at which your litters will produce, on average, the same range of characteristics. And if, at any time, a very specific selection pressure (like a human-controlled breeding program) is relaxed, the bell curve will likely ease back the other way.

104

Bottoming Out—Super-Mellow Dogs

It's possible that with dogs, natural and human selection over 15-135,000 years has already completed the Siberian Fox experiment, that the occurrence and intensity of aggression across the species is about as low as it can go. It seems more likely that we can push the bell curve a bit farther toward the affiliative end of the continuum, but there will always be a range of behavior among the members of any species. We won't know, of course, unless we implement a scrupulous policy of eliminating all threatening or biting or injuring (take your pick) individuals from the gene pool.

But trying to weed all aggressive behavior toward humans out of the dog population is probably useless. What we really need to study are the seriously injurious bites. This is certainly the most obvious road to isolating factors that actually increase the likelihood bites that hurt people.

It may be, for example, that the probability of injury is increased or decreased by the response of the person who is growled or snarled or snapped at. Perhaps some bites occur when people don't back off from dogs' warning signals, or as a trainer friend of mine calls them, "Please don't make me bite you" signals. Or not. Or it may be that the likelihood of harmful biting goes up in proportion to the number of the dog's growling incidents. Or it may go down. We don't know. What we do know, of course, is that intensive socialization of puppies can prevent a large proportion of neophobia-based biting, i.e., growling, snarling, snapping at, and finally biting, strangers.

The Canadian study included some mildly unexpected findings on which dogs are at slightly elevated risk for biting people they know well. Among these were small dogs (under 45 pounds), females in general, and dogs that had been treated for smelly, inflamed skin maladies.

The most interesting information from this study, though, is that less than 10 percent of the biting dogs actually injured anyone seriously enough so that they sought medical treatment, and these injuries were seldom severe. Guy and her colleagues found nothing that would help distinguish the damaging (defined as having delivered bites that received medical treatment) from the harmless biters, not even the size of the dogs. And needless to say, the group included no fatal bites. Even if it were possible for a person to keep a dog after such an incident, the sample size would need to be at least 5 million to have much chance of capturing just one.

So, since dogs almost never kill people, and they don't actually bite us very often, and when they do, we're seldom injured, and when we are, it's seldom serious, the only real question is whether we can do anything to further reduce the already small population of dogs that bite hard when they are upset enough to bite. This might be done through selective breeding or through changing rearing and training practices, or both. Finally, if we can reduce bites in these ways, what if anything should be the role of public policy in encouraging this?

CHAPTER SIX

Asking the Wrong Questions and Answering Them Badly: The Current State of Research on Biting Dogs

L et's say you want to know whether some people are more likely to get divorced than others. So you call a bunch of people and ask them a lot of questions about their best friends, including, naturally, whether they've been divorced and a lot of other stuff that you happen to think might be likely to incline people toward divorcing, including astrological signs. You discover that among the friends of the people you called, more Virgos seem to be getting divorced than say, Pisces.

Now, of course, you have no idea how many of the people you interviewed don't actually know where various signs fall on the calendar, or have forgotten when the friend's birthday is, or don't know when the friend's birthday is but think they remember somebody referring to the friend as a Virgo, or are having some fun with you, or are just plain guessing. In fact, if they're not sure, you ask for their best guess. You make no effort to verify their identification of the hapless Virgos.

You also don't know how many Virgos there are out there relative to people born under other signs. Nevertheless, you begin merrily speculating that since you already know from various authorities that Virgos are very meticulous, it must be that their poor spouses probably just can't put up with all that compulsive neatness and throw them over.

This is pretty much the state of research on the rate of dog bites by breed. Since in addition to being the most egregiously flawed category of dog-bite research, it's arguably the one that results in the most harm, it's worth considering first.

Breed Identification Follies

One such attempt to identify biting dogs by breed was conducted by studying dog bites reported to authorities in Denver in 1991. The researchers' most widely reported finding was that Chow Chows and German Shepherds were at increased risk for delivering an injurious bite relative to other breeds in the study.

The breed identification process used, however, is problematic. First, it was based on owner identification of the breed. It requires no more than a few trips to the local dog park to realize that people's identification of their dogs' breeds is haphazard at best. Even people with registered, pedigreed dogs often get it wrong, e.g., the woman in one of my classes recently who thought her American Eskimo was a Shi Tzu, or the people down the street who refer to their Shar Peis as Pit Bulls.

Figure12. People Confuse Breeds

American Eskimo

Shi Tzu

Shar Pei

Pit Bull Terrier

Moreover, purebred dogs (or at least dogs acquired from breeders) make up at most 29 percent of the dog population according to a 2002 survey by the American Pet Products Manufacturers Association. So the Denver researchers came up with the idea that when the interview subject identified the dog as a mix, they would record it as whatever the owner considered the "predominant" breed. Is easy to see the exponential increase in misidentification this would create.

It's likely to lead to a whopping number of dogs identified as German Shepherd Dogs, for example. Indeed, according to the data here, they must be as popular as Labrador Retrievers in Denver. Odd, since Labs currently outnumber GSD's in AKC registration by three to one.

The other most common misidentification is Pit Bull, but since they have been banned in Denver since 1989, nobody's likely to volunteer this identification over the phone to a stranger. The study was limited to dogs that had been with their owners at least six months, had not bitten before the reported incident, had bitten a non-household member who received medical treatment for the bite, and whose owners put their phone numbers on the report. This narrowed the study to about one-third of the reported dog bites for the year, and only about half of these identified cases could actually be interviewed. So finally, the study actually covered only 18 percent of the reported bites for the year.

It borders on the absurd to try to make a case for this as representative of biting dogs even in a single city, particularly since various studies have concluded that at most somewhere between five and ten percent of dog bites are ever reported. Astonishingly, while acknowledging most of these weaknesses themselves, including admitting that there was no statistically significant correlation between Chows and bites to children, these researchers still recommended that vets counsel their clients against acquiring Chows and German Shepherds, especially if they have kids. They didn't go so far as to recommend banning dogs by breed—no reputable researchers do. This is left to others.

Various insurance companies merrily took this data and began refusing to sell homeowner's insurance to owners of Chows and German Shepherds. Some even started excluding Akitas, of which there were five in the study! Some ban Dobermans, not represented in this study at all; the only studies that cite them are decades old. There's no way to know how many dogs who had been living their lives in loving homes were killed as a result. The findings on breeds and fatal dog attacks are even worse.

Breed Characteristics Over Time:
Trying To Draw A Morphing Target

Compiled by a panel of public health specialists and vets and published in the Journal of the American Veterinary Medical Association in 2000, the one major dog bite fatality study with regard to specific breeds purports to show an overrepresentation of Pit Bulls, Rottweilers, and German Shepherds.

The biggest problem here, of course, is that it just doesn't make sense to try to generalize about anything are rare as dog-bite fatalities. It takes a couple of decades for enough of these events to occur to permit statistically viable study. This is a very long time, genetically speaking, for a species that is reproductively viable at a less than a year of age. In fact, it didn't take much longer than this for Balyaev to transform his ferocious wild foxes into cuddly pets. Certainly, the behavioral characteristics of an already domesticated species like dogs could change in almost direction over such a period.

Even within the tiny, restricted gene pools that make up most pedigreed dog breeds, if you look at photos of winning dogs, you'll usually see significant (sometimes dramatic) changes over

111

a decade, certainly over two. And these changes are based on selection alone, without the introduction of any new individuals, much less other breeds, into the pool.

So the Cattle Dogs and Shelties have shrunk, and the Bulldogs' and Rottweilers' heads have gotten so big some of the puppies have to be delivered by Caesarian section, and Labradors are fatter and lower slung, and several breeds have been divided into separate English and American breeds, and so on. Aside from some behaviors that are persistent species wide—killing people is emphatically not one of these among domestic dogs—genetically driven characteristics are just too plastic to generalize about over this kind of time frame.

If It's Blond, It Must Be A Golden

The fatality findings with regard to breed completely collapse under the weight of unreliable breed identification. First, there was no information at all as to breed in more than one-third of the fatality cases, a very big hole in the data. Even more problematic, the identifications were made largely on the basis of newspaper reports, hardly reassuring.

The breed identification protocol here was much worse than even the Denver bite study cited above. Dogs' breeds were identified by all manner of witnesses, including bystanders, some of whom were children, police and animal control personnel. To give you sense of how reliable such information might be, think back to the news stories described above. In the case of the woman who was bitten while breaking up a fight between her Akita and a purported Pit Bull, the reporter went to the trouble of checking photos in a breed book. He concluded that an Akita was a breed that looked "like a German Shepherd."

The samples below can give you an idea of the appearances of the two breeds. Apparently, anything largish and canine, with a coat longer than a Rottweiler's, looks "like a German Shepherd!"

Figure 13

Akita   German Shepherd Dog

Clearly, one cannot assume that the average person can easily make clear discriminations based on the physical attributes of dogs, even when he can compare them to photos of bona fide examples of a breed. And a reporter, presumably, is a more skilled observer than the average person.

With regard to Pit Bulls, the fatality report doesn't even attempt to specify an actual breed. The designation is simply "Pit-Bull type" dogs, which, inexplicably, appear in both the "purebred" and "crossbred" categories.

The difficulties associated with using the terms "breed," and "Pit Bull" in the same phrase will be discussed further in the next chapter, but it's sufficient to say that at this point, in both the shelter and media worlds, pretty much any short-coated dog of medium-to-large size and either a stocky muscular body or a head

113

with a shorter muzzle or wider jaw than the average Labrador is labeled a Pit Bull. Unless it's black and tan, in which case we call it a Rottweiler. Unless it has a longer coat or sticky-up ears, in which case we call it a Shepherd cross regardless of body type or head shape. Unless it has a curled tail and/or one or two blue eyes, in which case it's called a Husky. (This last probably requires increasing the level of observer sophistication one dubious notch.)

The potential breed combinations (not even bringing mixed-breed dogs into it) that could result in these appearances makes the possible combinations in a super lotto drawing look small. The likelihood of being able to use them to predict genetic predisposition to particular behavior is, to put it mildly, remote. Given the huge percentage of dogs "identified" as Shepherds or Pits or Rotts, it's hardly a surprise that they would be the top three cited in a bite study. The correlation is about as viable as trying to pinpoint human nationality based on hair color with nothing to go on but hair color.

For a 1997–98 subreport, the same researchers solemnly point out that 67 percent of the 27 dog-bite deaths in that two-year period involved Pit Bulls or Rottweilers. Of course the writers were cheating a bit by their own rules here, since the reason for studying decades rather than a couple of years in the first place was that the short-term numbers were too small to be statistically viable. The most rudimentary understanding of statistics teaches one to beware of percentages that are larger than the actual raw numbers, e.g., where 16 cases become 67 percent.

Then they declare, while generously acknowledging some problems with the data, that "it is extremely unlikely that they (Pits and Rotties) accounted for anywhere near 60 percent of dogs in the United States during that same period." This is pure opinion, however, based on the assumption that AKC registration figures can be extrapolated to reflect rough percentages of particular breeds in the overall dog population.

Such extrapolation is really a stretch, at least with regard to Pits. In 2003 alone, 6,500 dogs identified as Pits went through the New York City shelter system alone, as compared to 1,600 American Staffordshire Terrier puppies (two-tenths of one percent of all registered puppies) registered with the AKC in the whole country for the same year. Since 35–50 percent and more of dogs going through most public shelter systems in recent years are identified as Pit Bulls (without even bringing the Rottweilers into it), I could just as easily argue that dogs of this description actually represent a huge percentage of the overall dog population. I do not make such a claim, of course, since I have a healthy respect for confounding variables. This respect is apparently not widely shared.

I'll Bet You Thought Someone Was Counting Dog-Bite Injuries
Let's leave the question of which dog breeds bite people most often for a bit and consider the larger research picture. Overall, two major questions are addressed in much of what is usually cited in the popular media as established research findings about dog bites. The first is how often dogs bite, including whether and how this has changed over time. The second is which dogs bite, either in terms of dog demographics, owner demographics, and owner or victim behavior.

Now one of the basic requirements for any research finding to become generally accepted is for various scientists to conduct the same research independently and come up with the same or similar results. In both areas of dog-bite research, the results are so widely disseminated that it's easy to imagine that such replication has taken place and that dog bites have been widely and thoroughly studied. This couldn't be farther from the truth. There is a kind of blind men describing the elephant grab bag of studies that has accumulated over time. But these are generally limited either geographically or according to a small aspect of the phenomenon studied.

Changing The Strike Zone In The Fifth Inning

The national numbers that you see over and over are the ones addressing the first question—how many dog bite injuries occur—and are the result of a handful of one-time studies. Even worse, the only two large studies of numbers of annual injuries from dog bites are often cited as evidence of an alarming increase (36 percent) simply because the one that came up with the larger number was conducted eight years after the one with the smaller. These two studies were conducted in completely different ways. They even defined injuries differently. One came up with 585,000 dog bite injuries per year; the other 800,000. You might decide to make a case for one being more valid than the other, but you simply cannot use them as evidence of change.

And there are other problems. Of course all these studies are based on samples. Now without sampling, the only way to get information about the incidence of anything would be to go around and knock on every door in the country and ask your questions, like the government does every 10 years in the big census. So everyone accepts that statistical findings can't yield certainty.

What's The Opposite Of A Sure Thing?

Statisticians have come up with ways to quantify the uncertainty. One term for it is confidence interval, which is basically a range of statistically plausible numbers. What a confidence interval tells you is the range of results you'd expect to get if you collected your data over and over, using the same methodology. So a small confidence interval means that the range of plausible values is small: you have a lot of confidence in your result. A large one means just the opposite.

On the two injury studies described above, the ranges are very large indeed. For example for the 1994 study that concluded that 800,000 people had been treated for dog bites, the statistically plausible range was 345,039 to 1,168,363! Again, what this means is that a statistician would be really surprised if the same study were redone in the same way and came up with a total less that 345,000 or more than 1,168,000. Anything in between would be all in a day's work. For the 1986 study which liked the 585,000 result, the range was 226,000 to 944,000. Basically, we're in the "give or take three quarters of a million" range.

A Light In The Data Wilderness—
Emergency Department Records

In fact, the only fully replicated ongoing data collection regarding dog bites is that done in hospital Emergency Departments (ED). The two reports on these data (one compiled from hospital reports in 1994 and the other in 2001 by the National Center for Injury Prevention and Control department of the CDC) show a tiny one-percent increase in dog-bite injuries during that seven-year period. However, during the same period, all estimates of the overall domestic-dog population show increases. And while the

117

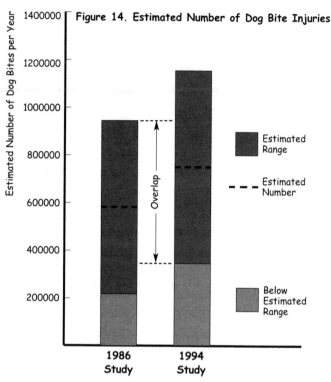

Figure 14. Estimated Number of Dog Bite Injuries

A comparison between these two studies is often touted as proof that the annual number of injurious dog bites in the US has increased by 36 percent from 585,000 in 1986 to 756,701 (rounded off as 800,000) in 1994. These data may seem impressive, but they are merely estimates (educated guesses) based on a very small sample size. The 1986 estimate of 585,000 was based on just six dog bites, and the 1994 estimate was based on 38. Estimating big numbers from very little ones is wildly inaccurate and so, statisticians calculate a range of plausible values. The smaller the range, the more likely the estimates are close to correct. The larger the range, the more likely the estimates are incorrect. Because these annual estimates were based on so few dog bites, the ranges are huge and they overlap considerably. Consequently, comparing data from these two studies tells us nothing about whether dog bites have increased, decreased, or remained the same. The margin of possible error in both these studies makes the typical political poll look precise.

confidence intervals for these studies are certainly narrow enough to, well, inspire confidence, they are still wide enough to overlap each other: one percent is after all a very narrow margin. In other words, statistically speaking, there may quite plausibly have been no increase in dog bite injuries at all.

The data collection method here certainly inspires more confidence in other ways, as it's based on events directly reported on hospital admissions records. These injuries are actually documented. All the other studies rely on people's memory and truthfulness and just plain willingness to respond to questions about events that were medically treated or led to restricted activity. The ED data has the added advantage of being likely to catch most of the serious injuries—ER's are where people usually go for these. Further, the typical dog-bite injury is dramatically less severe than the general levels of injury presented in ED's.

While the ED data certainly cannot capture all medically treated dog bites, they may well capture nearly all the ones worth worrying about. In fact, the injuries from most dog-bite cases are so minor they would never be recorded anywhere had they occurred in any other way. Unfortunately, dog-bite cases involving little or no injury are lumped with the extremely rare serious cases. Hardly the makings of a crisis.

News Flash—Don't Try To Pat The Dog
That's Snarling At You On The End Of A Chain

So much for how many people are bitten by dogs. How about the question of which dogs are doing the biting? The Denver study attempts to address this. As discussed earlier, the study has serious weaknesses as a sample generalizable to any large population of biting dogs. The specific demographic and behavioral questions it addresses probably have a better chance of being answered accurately than the breed identification questions. Unfortunately, these don't yield very much that suggest changes that might prevent dog bites.

The researchers found that the biting dogs in the study were more likely to be chained up than the non-biting dogs, for example, but this in no way suggests that the chaining caused the biting. It may suggest that it's not a good idea to approach a dog you don't know if it's chained up, but let's face it, this is pretty much Darwin Award behavior to begin with. Biting dogs were more likely to live with kids, so should families with children not have dogs, or people with dogs not have kids?

Biting The Hand That Feeds You And Biting The Stranger That Grabs You Are Different Animals

You may recall that the Denver study was limited to dogs that had bitten "non-household members." These dogs were matched with a control group of dogs that had never bitten such a person. One interesting finding is reminiscent of Sherlock Holmes' observation of the clue of the "the dog that did not bark in the night." Both groups of dogs (non-household member biters and controls) nipped and bit household members at exactly the same rate. And they were equally likely (well within the statistical margin of error) to growl and snap at visitors and to bark at passers by.

This suggests that growling and snapping at visitors doesn't predict actually biting them. It might also suggest that dogs that bite strangers, maybe even strangers they encounter in public, may be no more or less likely to bite familiar people than those that don't bite strangers. Unfortunately, the non-household member

120

classification can include both familiar and unfamiliar people, so we just can't tell. So at the end of the day, the most widely cited study on which dogs bite suffers from a sample that is not convincingly representative and variables that just aren't very useful. The whole thing is pretty hopeless.

As mentioned in the previous chapter, there are a couple of studies out there that hold promise for approaches that may yield useful information on the question of which dogs are most likely to bite. One study of over 2,000 dogs (in The Journal of Applied Animal Welfare Science) involved dog owners completing a carefully worded questionnaire about the frequency of 127 very specific behaviors in their dogs. The researchers, behaviorists Goodloe and Borchelt, found, unsurprisingly, that dogs that growled and snarled in response to being handled and restrained or being approached while eating were more likely to bite their owners than those who didn't.

The Doberman Head On The Pillow—Asking For Trouble?
On the other hand, the study debunked some of the widespread conventional wisdom about dogs, finding that playing tug-of-war or other rough games was not connected with increased likelihood of any aggressive behavior, nor was sleeping on the owner's bed.

They also found, interestingly, that warning signals like growling were less predictive of biting when the target was strangers than when the dogs growled at their own people.

Now this study did not pretend or even attempt to be a representative sample of dogs, nor to establish causal links among behaviors. The purpose was simply to try to determine what behaviors tend to go together.

The Canadian study mentioned earlier (led by Guy of Atlantic Veterinary College and Luescher of Purdue) is probably the most representative large-scale study of pet dogs done to date, including data on over 3,000 dogs, 84 percent of all the clients who crossed the thresholds of 20 veterinary clinics in three Canadian provinces over a month's time.

The findings with regard to which dogs bite were somewhat disappointing in terms of prevention strategies. Small spayed females were found to bite a little more often than males or intact females. Other slightly likely suspects were dogs living in households with teenagers, and ones who had been receiving veterinary treatment for really nasty itchy-burny skin disorders.

The researchers could only speculate as to the links between biting and these factors. Skin disorders in dogs, for example, are commonly treated with corticosteroids like Prednisone which have been previously shown to increase irritability and aggression in some dogs. Moreover, the skin infections themselves might well elicit irritable aggression, especially in the context of often painful treatment.

What is most useful to remember, though, is simply how common they found noninjurious aggression to be, with 41 percent having growled or snarled at a family member or other person the dog knew well. Yet only 15 percent had actually bitten, and only 9 percent of those (or roughly 1 percent of the dogs overall), had bitten hard enough to produce an injury for which medical attention was sought.

They also found that owners are more likely to rank as serious a bite delivered by a large male even though the injuries from these

122

bites were typically no more serious than bites from females or smaller dogs. This may explain some of the data that's frequently cited claiming males as the most frequent culprits and large dogs as doing the most damage.

Intriguingly, in a study that presumably included the input of at least one veterinarian regarding breed identification, this study found that Golden Retrievers bit household members as frequently as did German Shepherds.

What we can say so far is that many if not most dogs, like many if not most humans, threaten from time to time, whether the threat is a growl or a snarl or a raised voice. But few dogs actually bite, probably fewer than humans who actually hit. Fewer still, as with humans, cause serious injury.

We might know more if a study like Guy and Luescher's could be expanded to include bites to strangers and the kind of detailed human-dog interaction scenarios of the Goodloe and Borchelt research. We might then get some documentation of the kinds of situations that are most problematic. We could then breed and train dogs that could tolerate these situations well.

In the meantime, the worst data is the most publicized and leads to poorly conceived public policies, with tragic results for many dogs and the people who love them.

CHAPTER SEVEN

For Every Complex Problem There Is A Simple Solution. And It Is Wrong: Dog Bite Legislation

There may be some things worth trying if we want to decrease the incidence of injurious dog bites. Dangerous-dog laws as presently envisioned are not among them. There is simply no reason to suppose that current approaches to dangerous-dog legislation will do anything to decrease injurious dog bites. There are currently two main approaches to this kind of legislation. One is based on morphology, the other on evidence of aggressive behavior.

The first approach to dangerous-dog laws is clearly the more dangerous and so will be considered first. This is, of course, the breed bans. There are many reasons why such legislation has no hope of addressing the issue. I'll consider the two I find most compelling here.

As we have seen in the previous chapter, the evidence presented for implicating specific breeds in fatalities and injuries to people is hopelessly flawed. We might as well go back to phrenology as a way to predict criminal behavior in humans. Interestingly, not a single reputable conductor of such research recommends breed bans as a solution, but researchers clearly bear some of the responsibility for this development.

If You're Blond, You Must Be Swedish

I once knew a quirky, sweet-tempered, Nordic-looking dog called Fred, who was fond of fishing ice cubes out of people's drinks, yodeling, and pooping on vertical surfaces. People, even Malamute people, would often compliment me on what a handsome specimen of the breed he was. Now I knew both of Fred's parents: his mother the Samoyed and his father the Rough Collie (that's the Lassie kind). There is absolutely no reason to suppose that Fred shared any more DNA with a Malamute than with, say, a Beagle.

Admittedly, Fred was an extreme case. It is in fact often possible to visually identify an individual as a likely (never certain) member of a given breed, if it satisfies the elaborate set of precise physical characteristics of that breed's description, especially if some of those characteristics (or combinations of characteristics) are either unique in themselves or simply unlikely to occur in combination by chance. But this only applies to pedigreed dogs, and then only to those who are closely related to show animals whose breeders are selecting for characteristics that conform to the breed description, a practice much like trying to hold water in a colander. Once you include backyard-bred or puppy-mill dogs, anything can happen.

126

Visual breed identification, short of actual AKC records, is extremely problematic. You may as well assume that two humans of similar height, bone structure, and pigmentation are related as to assume that two dogs that generally resemble each other are members of the same breed.

One of the most pervasive examples of this in the dog world is German Shepherd Dogs. Those of us who work with dogs tend to cavalierly label pretty much any black-and-tan dog (unless it has a very flat face or an extremely short coat) as a GSD cross. This is part of the casual parlor game we play, trying to guess mixed-breed dogs' backgrounds generally. Curiously, we almost always hypothesize only two breeds (or a single "predominant" one) in a given dog's background! Obviously, unless nearly all crossbred dogs were eliminated in the first generation, it is vastly more likely that the forebears of any mixed-breed dog have dipped into many genetic pools.

You don't need more than a vague memory of the stuff you learned in high school about the geneticist Gregor Mendel and his fruit flies to understand that there are a lot of routes to similar appearance. So I assume (or at least I hope) that most of us are throwing around the "German Shepherd cross" identification as a kind of rough shorthand description (meaning mixed-breed dog that resembles a German Shepherd) not as an actual hypothesis about ancestry.

But inevitably insider shorthand becomes conventional wisdom. It's certainly likely that this kind of convenience labeling bleeds over into supposedly literal breed identification. This may well account for the purported "overrepresentation" of German

Shepherds and German Shepherd crosses among dog-bite statistics. Overreporting is more likely.

And this problem is especially extreme with regard to the most commonly legislated against dogs, the so called Pit Bulls. There are enormous numbers of animals that bear some resemblance to the actual breeds usually categorized as Pits. The selection process of these dogs is completely undocumented. There is simply no way to predict any increased likelihood of aggression (much less injurious bites), especially toward humans, based on a superficial resemblance to, say, an American Staffordshire Terrier.

Including the Bull Terrier and the Staffordshire Terrier) in such legislation is just plain silly. Both are relatively rare but very recognizable breeds. The Bull Terrier sports an extremely distinctive Roman-nosed profile and the Staffordshire a very small physique. Neither bears much resemblance to the dogs paraded around by young males in tough neighborhoods.

There are a tiny number (about 1,600 puppies per year) of actual AKC registered American Staffordshire Terriers (the breed that does fit the usual Pit Bull physical image). But at this point these pedigreed AmStaffs are probably not much more aggressive even toward dogs than, say, Bulldogs and Boxers, since the AKC itself has wisely instituted very stiff penalties for even a whisper of dog-fighting activity among breeders.

Moreover, this same general appearance would be the likely result of crossing any of the many Mastiff-type breeds with any short-coated breed or a Boxer with just about anything less squashed-nosed. That's just the obvious two breed combinations. Many others would produce a Pit Bull-esque physique. Completely unrelated dogs, like completely unrelated people, often resemble one another.

Some interesting research has recently shown some promise of identifying the breed ancestry of mixed-breed dogs. No one is suggesting, however, that they're close to linking specific genes to particular behavioral tendencies. In any case, nobody is proposing looking to DNA testing for breed-ban documentation.

Most of the breed ban statutes have language like Denver's mind-boggling "any dog that is an American Pit Bull Terrier, American Staffordshire Terrier, Staffordshire Bull Terrier, or any dog displaying the majority of physical traits of any one (1) or more of the above breeds, or any dog exhibiting those distinguishing characteristics which substantially conform to the standards established by the American Kennel Club or United Kennel Club for any of the above breeds."

I don't know what is meant by a dog that "is" one of these breeds, apart from displaying the physical characteristics of the breed. Perhaps this refers to registered dogs that are so carelessly bred that they don't look anything like the breed standard. But in terms of "displaying the majority of traits of one," the AKC lists no fewer than 59 physical traits for the AmStaff.

I'm assuming, of course, that the traits referred to are physical ones, as the behavioral traits described in the breed standards, include things like, "confidence, zest for life," "eager to please," "love of children," etc. Banning dogs exhibiting such traits would be, to say the least, bizarre.

129

You can find 30 or so ("a majority") of these traits in dogs ranging from Dalmatians to Labs to Boston Terriers to Dobermans. The same holds true for the APBT's and Staffies. Moreover, it's a mathematical impossibility for any dog to "display the majority of physical traits" of more than one of these breeds. There's not enough overlap in the breed standards. So what that part of the ban means is anybody's guess. It's never a good thing, though, when any legislation casts a net so wide it can be stretched to catch almost anybody.

Certainly, there are criminals who are finding dogs of with various combinations of these physical traits and selectively breeding them for dog-dog aggression. And there are idiots breeding for neophobia. Now while this latter probably ought to be a crime rather than being just stupid, it's hardly unique to this kind of dog—remember the Caucasian Mountain Dog enthusiasts.

Swimming Against The Evolutionary Tide
Both the fighting dog and spooky dog breeders are swimming against the evolutionary tide of the species. For most of the last 15,000 to 135,000 years the adaptive pressure has been largely toward less intense aggression rather than more. (There are currently two conflicting DNA studies hypothesizing different timelines for the domestication of dogs, hence the wide date range.) Unfriendly dogs and ones that hurt people have generally been culled.

What this means is that it's now pretty easy to breed for more aggression because the behavioral envelope extends farther in that direction. What's difficult is to keep aggression high, requiring consistent breeding standards. Unless you keep up the selective pressure, individuals will tend to normalize around the human friendly median for the species. Plainly, however, many people, no brighter than those who put in place the breed bans, are breeding dogs for "Pit Bull" appearance, because they can sell the puppies to uninformed, ill-intentioned people, based on public image. And clearly the population of dogs of this description has exploded during the period since breed ban legislation has become widespread.

So the legislation itself enhances the mythologized image of these dogs as super aggressive, thus increasing their attraction for people who like this idea, and who are precisely those people most likely to treat them inappropriately and encourage aggression. Nobody, anywhere, thinks there are fewer Pitties around than before breed-ban legislation began.

But let's imagine a fantasy universe where we actually could reliably identify a group of genetically closely related dogs as Pit Bulls, and that we could determine how many of them there were, and that it turned out that a larger percentage of them were biting and hurting people than were dogs of other breeds, and that we could determine that this propensity to injure was not simply the result of malicious or incompetent husbandry or training methods. Let's say that we could find a way to enforce a ban on them. This last may be the most absurd of our conditions since the resources to effectively enforce such a ban would not only be prohibitively expensive, they would necessitate civil rights abuses that even our current cultural mood would not likely put up with.

But just for the sake of our alternate universe, let's say we could eliminate all these dogs. Here's the bottom line.

It wouldn't make any difference.

Cujofying Snoopy

You just don't need much brainpower to breed scrappy dogs. You don't even need a lot of time or resources. All anybody so inclined (and clearly some people are) would need to do would be to pick the scrappiest pups from litters of any breed at all and mate them with similarly reactive individuals. If they were really serious about breeding for aggression rather than just the image, in other words the substance rather than just packaging, they'd go for a wide range of physical appearance to make things more difficult for the dog police. We'd be back to square one in three to five years at the most.

It goes without saying that deliberate undersocialization and agitation of dogs for the purpose of maximizing aggression can be carried out with any breed. You just take responsible puppy raising principles and reverse them. A dog's violent potential is unquestionably intensified if she meets few people as a puppy. And if she is repeatedly pushed and threatened into growling, snarling, snapping, and biting, and then rewarded for this behavior, she will growl, snarl, snap, and bite more readily. While it's a gross distortion to refer to any dog as a "fuzzy gun," any dog can learn to be a biter. It's a whole lot easier to manufacture a hyper-aggressive dog in your backyard than to make a gun out of your home toolbox.

Homo sapiens—The Most Dangerous Biting Breed?

The only study so far on pre- and post-breed-ban–dog-bite rates was completed in the UK in the mid 1990's. The study concluded that the Dangerous Dogs Act had had no effect whatever. The Aberdeen Royal Infirmary researchers did find, however that "human bites were as common as those from the most implicated dog breed." People bite as much as any breed of dog.

And these are just the reported bites. They certainly don't include incidents like the one described to me recently: a "level 3 bite" (from the bite severity scale developed by Dr. Ian Dunbar—a 3 is bruises and broken skin) delivered to a mom through her shirt by her 10-month-old son who has three and one-half teeth. Yet another tsk tsk for those who fuss over how slack we all are about reporting bites to the proper authorities.

Bad Laws Corrupt Law Enforcement And Citizens Alike

Perhaps the most insidious problem with all such legislation, however, is the potential for abuse. This is always the case when laws exist without the practical means to widely enforce them. The result is selective enforcement, enforcement based on grudge complaints, and perhaps most worrisome, driving the behavior underground.

Not only can this make criminals of otherwise law-abiding people, it is not farfetched to think that people hiding their dogs from the authorities could increase the risk of zoonotic disease. Up until the mid 20th century, about 100 Americans per year died of rabies for example; today it's one or two and in some years none. Not one of these deaths has been the result of a domestic-animal bite in decades. This is entirely attributable to the very high rate of vaccination of domestic dogs against this disease. We would be ill-advised to do anything that would discourage anybody from inoculating their dogs against rabies.

Doggy Parole

The only faintly encouraging finding anywhere in terms of potential impact on dog-bite injuries through legislation was an Oregon study that showed a drop in repeated injurious bites (from 25 percent down to 7 percent) among 422 dogs whose owners had

had restrictions placed on them after the first bite. Since the study did not include a control group, further research would be required to make sure that it was the restrictions rather than simply increased caution on the part of people whose dogs had injured someone that accounted for the decrease. But it is suggestive that such a doggy parole system might well have prevented the 2001 San Francisco fatality, as one of the dogs involved had previously seriously bitten one of the owners on the hand.

Finding the resources to keep an eye on compliance of roughly half-a-million dog owners per year is probably an insurmountable obstacle to real world implementation of such a system, however. Certainly, the results of parole system attempts to track behavior restrictions on human criminals are not encouraging. Still, this study is unique in finding something that had a measurable effect on the incidence of dog bites. If we are serious about decreasing dog-bite injury, it provides a sensible model to try.

Rap Sheets—Better Than Psychic Readings (Sort Of)
This may suggest that the other major approach to dangerous-dog law is at least more rational than breed bans. This approach targets the behavior of the individual dog, designating a particular dog with a label like "potentially dangerous," "dangerous" or in some cases "vicious," based on actual incidents and then limiting the conditions under which the dog can be kept.

So a dog that has bitten and injured a child at the park, to use a very straightforward example, might be required to be leashed and muzzled at all times when in public and when visitors come into the home. In cases where the dog is deemed to present an extreme hazard, it can be removed from the home and killed.

134

As with breed bans, however, there are many of these statutes at both municipal and state levels, and they use a dizzying variety of approaches to defining dangerous animals.

Perhaps this muddle is inevitable, since many dangerous-dog laws try not only to control dogs that have already injured people, but to predict which ones will do so in the future and attempt to prevent this. Any such approach generally fails to recognize the pervasiveness of low-level aggression among dogs. Look into pretty much any dog's history closely enough, and you'll find some evidence of aggression. Most dogs, as discussed earlier, growl or snarl or snap at someone at some time.

Dangerous-dog laws are rife with fuzzy descriptions such as: "approaches in a vicious or terrorizing manner" or "in a menacing fashion"; or has "a known disposition, tendency, or propensity to attack." Some require only that the dog "endangered" a person in some way, leaving the way open for complaints by anyone who simply felt endangered.

My own state, California, may take the prize for haziness in defining as dangerous a dog that "engages in any behavior that requires a defensive action by any person to prevent bodily injury." A dog who runs into the street causing a car to swerve would qualify under this definition. If he did it twice, this dog would be certified "vicious."

Inconsistencies abound. Crossing state and county lines can render a dog dangerous. Some statutes include dogs that injure or kill other domestic animals; some don't. Some exclude bites that occur on the owner's property; some don't.

Taking A Bite Out Of Crime (Or At Least Criminals)

Most dangerous dog statutes include the worrisome concept of "unprovoked" threat or bite behaviors, with few clearly defining provocation. Of course, from the dog's perspective, all bites are provoked.

Whether or not she's inclined to bite a person is going to depend upon the dog's socialization history, on which people and interactions she learned to see as benign as a puppy. Socialization determines whether the dog perceives a given human as friend, foe, or playmate. Most human definitions of exculpatory provocation completely fail to take into consideration the fact that there is always a perceived threat from the dog's point of view if he growls or snarls or snaps or bites.

Misguided human lawmakers simply transpose acts that would be defined as justifiable for humans onto dogs. So some definitions of provocation include bites when the person bitten was "committing a willful trespass or other tort," or "was committing or attempting to commit a crime." These are particularly interesting, as we must infer from them either that it's okay to keep a dog that's inclined to bite as long as you only let it bite trespassers and criminals, or that dogs themselves can somehow tell when people are committing crimes.

Some statutes exclude bites when the dog was "protecting" the owner. Some imply a definition of provocation by excluding bites where the victim "was tormenting, abusing, or assaulting the dog, [or] had tormented, abused, or assaulted the dog." This point implies that a dog may be allowed to preemptively bite someone it has learned to fear or dislike because of past mistreatment.

It's crucial to any hope of fair enforcement that designations like "dangerous" be both reasonable and precise. Not only are owners of dogs so labeled required to confine their pets in elaborately described ways, they are increasingly subject to felony criminal charges if the dog subsequently bites and injures someone.

It is possible to define concepts like provocation with some precision. New York City, for example, specifies that "'unprovoked" means that the dog was "not hit, kicked, taunted or struck by a person with any object or part of a person's body nor was any part of the dog's body pulled, pinched or squeezed by a person." Now whether or not you agree that dogs should tolerate any kind of human behavior other than actual attacks on them, this is a clear standard of "provocation."

It's possible to have a law that identifies dogs that present a demonstrable threat to humans. Such a law would need to include clear standard of provocation like New York's. It would include a requirement that the dog actually injure someone. Unfortunately, this is seldom the case. Finally, it would need a clear definition of serious injury. Some statutes do include this. Such a law might even be equitably enforceable if medically treated bites were consistently reported.

But dangerous-dog laws are only one piece of the legislative puzzle. The issue of civil liability is even more difficult to unravel, which exacerbates one more kind of dread—lawsuit anxiety.

CHAPTER EIGHT

Another Cultural Phobia—"I Could Be Sued"

Human beings have evolved to feel the urge to strike out when we are hurt. So has the rest of the animal world. The fact of this impulse, however, does not necessarily mean that retribution by the state or by ourselves as individuals is always justified. I read most of Joseph LeDoux's book on the neurobiology of fear one evening while sitting in the emergency department of a busy urban hospital.

The kind ER nurse who was treating me for my minor heart ailment asked what I was reading. I briefly explained LeDoux's ideas about fear and the brain. I was writing a book, I told her, about dog bites, and I thought LeDoux offered an explanation for how much more upset people feel about dog bites than about other kinds of injuries. I shared with her my suspicion that people often seek medical treatment for very minor bites. She responded, matter-of-factly, "Don't you think they just want to get something out of it?"

139

This led me to participate, reluctantly, in the shopworn complaint that Shakespeare's Henry V should have heeded his drinking buddy's advice to "first kill all the lawyers." As it turns out, the blame probably belongs mostly to the insurance industry, the real arbiters of liability in this country.

The Last Legal Redlining

I recently met a man who's in the process of refinancing his house. One of the last steps was the routine process of transferring his insurance to the new lender. The insurance inspector took one look at his dog, said, "prohibited dog breed," refused to sign off on the loan papers, and cancelled his homeowner's insurance on the spot. His dog is a middle-aged female Rottweiler who's never bitten anyone, human or canine, and works as a therapy dog, frequently visiting frail, sick, and elderly people at a local convalescent hospital, comforting them with her gentle presence. It would have made as much sense to cancel the policy because of the swingset in the backyard, as play equipment injures and kills more children than dogs do, and certainly far more than any particular breed of dog.

In the 80's, I had a neighbor in a very modest neighborhood who for several years got her homeowner's insurance from Lloyds of London. Not because she had squirreled away a Van Gogh, or a twin to the Hope diamond, not because she wanted to pay a lot for a prestigious name on her insurance, but because her dog had bitten her teenage niece. The dog had been tethered in the corner of an upstairs bedroom and the girl told not to approach him, but she decided to go pet him anyway, whereupon he bit her in the face. After some minor plastic surgery, but before resuming her part-time modeling hobby, she sued her aunt, whose insurance company settled out of court for $40,000.

In the 90's, I lived in a fairly upscale area of Oakland where the houses are large and built on hillsides. One afternoon I heard barking and yelling out front and went to investigate. When I got down to the sidewalk, I found a woman sitting on the edge of the hill, weeping and holding her ankle. She was an interviewer for a survey I had agreed to participate in. This was her first visit, and inexplicably, instead of coming up the sidewalk, she had climbed the hill beside the garage and cut through the yard, where my landlady's dog was tied out. He woke up from napping in his dog house to find a stranger in the yard and bit her on the ankle. In addition, the woman scraped her knee in her scramble to get out of the dog's range. I drove her to the nearest hospital emergency room where her wound was treated and bandaged.

The animal control officer who came out the next day to investigate checked the dog's rabies and registration tags, looked around at the property, met the dog, and said, "Looks like he was just doing his job," and suggested my neighbor post a "Beware of dog" sign on the edge of the property. Of course, he might just as reasonably have suggested a "Beware of hillside" sign. In any case, that was that. No lawsuit, no insurance payout.

Now one of the interesting things about these two events is that they are the only dog bites requiring medical attention I know of among my acquaintances, outside of my professional dog-training life. This doesn't, of course, mean that nobody else I know has ever been injured by a dog, just that I haven't heard about it. Nor does it mean that my experience is typical, although I did find it amusing that in the course of an interview about insurance losses for dog bites, a chatty representative of an insurance public relations organization offered that she didn't know anybody who had ever been hurt by a dog. These are the sorts of things that make one suspect that the liability issue, like everything else about dog bites, has been blown out of proportion.

For one thing, we have more information about bad things that can happen than is good for us, or at least more than we can handle realistically. In other words, in the same way that publicity can create exaggerated fears of dog bites, it can also create exaggerated fears of being sued over a dog bite.

So the publicity given to the occasional huge lawsuit award (usually having to do with a dangerous product) and the seemingly large numbers of suits that are often cited lead to often unrealistic anxieties among individuals about being sued in mundane situations. A recent study by William Haltom and Michael McCann confirmed this. The two political science professors found that although the numbers of lawsuits filed has actually decreased in the last decade, the number of stories in the media about them has dramatically increased.

Not very many people who sustain injuries for which someone could reasonably be held liable file lawsuits at all. According to a Rand Institute survey of 28,000 households for the US Department of Health and Human Services, among people who sustain injuries, only 10 percent attempt to get compensation of any kind, including from their own health insurance. Only about two percent sue anyone. Only about half of those suits are successful.

Insurance Company Woes—Sheep In Wolf's Clothing?

Now the widespread insurance industry claim (compiled by the Insurance Information Institute) is that dog-bite claims cost them

THE LEGAL LIABILITY QUESTION

$321.6 million in 2004, down $24 million from 2003. They also claim a 38-percent (or 4–5 percent per year) increase in claims between 1995 and 2002. Their figures for 2003 work out to 20,813 paid claims per year.

Yet dog bites cost less per claim than other kinds of liability. The insurers' figures put the average dog-bite settlement at $16,600. The average liability settlement overall for everything from car accidents to falling on slippery floors is in the neighborhood of $38,000.

Even if we accept the insurance industry's dog-bite claim figures, they hardly warrant the insurers' draconian policies. The total amounts paid out are a tiny fraction of claims overall, about one-tenth of one percent. The industry's total costs for all bodily injury and property damage liability (including dog bites and slipping on the icy front porch steps and everything else) is only five percent of the total paid out on homeowner's claims. Total homeowner's claims have actually gone down more than two percent overall in the last seven years.

Liability insurance is basically just the frosting on the homeowner's insurance cake. The big ingredients are all in the property damage cupboard. These are losses like fire (24 percent) and weather and water damage (34 percent). Big natural disasters like hurricanes and newly publicized, widespread environmental hazards like mold and asbestos are where the homeowners' insurers really get bitten. Dog-bite claims, according to the insurers, account for about a quarter of the puny liability five percent. Dog-bite claims just aren't breaking the bank for insurers even by their own accounting. The most extravagant possible estimate would place dog-bite claims paid at about one percent of homeowners insurance payouts.

There is also the question of the reliability of the insurance-industry figures. The Insurance Information Institute's data collection procedure is casual, to say the least. According to a spokesperson for the Insurance Information Institute, it is based on voluntary reporting by individual companies on estimated amounts paid out on various categories of claims, with no standardization, published or otherwise, on how the data is collected. Not a process to inspire much expectation of accuracy, much less objectivity, especially when compiled by an extremely interested party.

The Real Pot Of Gold At The End Of The Liability Rainbow

Up to this point the universe is unfolding as it should. After all, this is what insurance is for, to protect you against some unexpected real bad luck. Fixing things that happen to your house, like floods, and fires, and unforeseen environmental hazards like mold in the basement are the main kinds of bad luck that homeowner's insurance protects you from and, of course, this is where the big costs to the insurance companies are, in the 10's of billions in a bad disaster year and making up the vast majority of claims in any year.

Insurance also protects you against the cost of a visitor getting hurt on your property, especially if they're badly hurt. One way a visitor can get hurt is to get bitten by your dog. Now this is certainly not the only way that people get hurt in their own or others' homes. Statistically, for example, slipping and falling is vastly more common, and more serious, but no one except the insurers themselves keeps track of liability claims for falls, and they're not telling.

I was baffled for some time as to why insurance companies were adopting such harsh policies regarding dog owners, refusing to insure some people and thereby sending their business elsewhere if they're not willing to kill their dogs. Now we have a possible answer: dog insurance.

In at least one state already, there has been an attempt to require all dog owners to carry special liability insurance against injuries resulting from a dog bite. A whole new product is a rare and wondrous thing in the insurance industry. This is one with a potential market of 30 to 40 million customers (the estimated number of households with dogs). It even expands the market beyond people who typically carry homeowners insurance, like many renters, as long as they have dogs. Now that would be a windfall.

At first glance, it almost seems like a good idea, a way out of the morass of the irrational, discriminatory policies that attempt to ferret out dangerous dogs for exclusion or higher rates. And it's a solution for the anxiety many people feel about losing their homeowner's insurance if the family dog bites somebody. It's the insurance companies' threats to cancel dog-owners' insurance that created the anxiety in the first place, but never mind. Of course, insurers could still refuse to cover specific breeds or anybody who has had a claim paid out or whatever struck their fancy.

It makes sense until you realize that what this would do is itemize risks that should be covered by people's regular insurance. The only other aspect of ordinary people's personal lives that is singled out in this way is driving, and cars kill 45,000 people and seriously injure 3.5 million more every year in this country and are the class of injury most likely to result in lawsuits and other liability claims. Dogs, on the other hand, kill about 15 people and injure perhaps a half a million.

It may be time to insist that offering protection (at a price) does not give the insurance industry the right to make basic life choices for us. While we're at it, why not require them to prove that the risks that they charge extra premiums for actually cost them proportional losses?

Admittedly, civil dog-bite liability standards are a mess. They are so bad, they make dangerous-dog statutes look orderly and consistent. Dog-bite cases are difficult to defend and sometimes result in inflated awards, creating something of a cottage industry for personal injury lawyers. A 30 minute Internet search will yield you dozens of law firms soliciting the business of dog bite victims, with come-ons like "your injury may be worth more than you think."

It may even be that people pursue lawsuits and insurance claims for dog bite injuries at a somewhat higher rate than for some others. This seems plausible. The Rand Institute study found that most people felt that they were themselves at least partly responsible for their (non work or auto-related) injuries or that it had been "just an accident" that "could have happened to anybody." When they felt this way, they were unlikely to instigate lawsuits. People are probably more likely blame someone when they are bitten by dogs, given the poverty of understanding of dog behavior.

Few people were found to seek compensation from avarice, but the temptation to do this with regard to dog bites is probably higher than the norm. The outcomes of dog-bite cases turn on muddled ideas about dog behavior, and they are often easy to win. Thus insurance companies readily settle. All this has given the insurance industry the opportunity to create a new market niche, supported only by their internal loss numbers, the sources of which are proprietary and thus secret.

Attack Cats—The Next Public Health Crisis?
My next-door neighbor has a cat who sometimes approaches visitors and rubs against them in the way cats do. My neighbor duly warns the visitor not to touch the cat. Some people attempt to stroke the critter anyway, and are immediately met with a flurry of biting and scratching.

"I've spent a lot of money at the ER over the years getting people stitched up," my neighbor said to me of his pet.

Oddly, we both seemed to find some amusement in these tales, he in the telling and me in listening, although it could easily be argued that cats are more dangerous than dogs. In recent years, for example, there have been twice as many cases of rabies in cats than in dogs, although, I hasten to add, no cases of human contraction of the disease from domestic animals has been traced to either species in the United States in decades.

People bitten by cats (perhaps I should say cat-bite victims) are six times more likely to need rabies prevention treatment than those bitten by dogs. This is because cats are less often immunized against the disease, and people often don't know who owns a cat

DOGS BITE: BUT BALLOONS AND SLIPPERS ARE MORE DANGEROUS

that bites them—not so with dogs. Also, cat bites are much more likely to result in complications from infection than are dog bites.

Where is the outcry over underreported cat bites? Occasionally, cat bites do results in lawsuits and insurance claims, but these seem to be resolvable without reference to special "Dangerous Cat" laws or insurance policies to cover them. It seems to me that the lack of general alarm over cat bites represents a rational view of a minor hazard of everyday life that we might do well to consider applying to dogs as well.

CHAPTER NINE

What Do We Want Dogs For, Anyway?

By the time my brother had reached the age of five, I could often hear his labored wheezing through the wall between our bedrooms as he struggled to breathe before he fell asleep at night. My mother would use a humidifier to try to soften the irritation to his bronchial tubes if he had happened to visit a house with a wool rug or ventured outside while someone was mowing a lawn. And he's had life-threatening encounters with lentils and other legumes. This is the same brother who my mother was protecting as an infant by getting rid of the jumping puppy, Tippy.

Cost/Benefit Analysis: Dogs Are Good For Kids After All

Recently in Sweden a very large study of children has shown a dramatically lower incidence of allergies among children who lived with a dog or a cat, preferably both, during the first year of life. That's the funny thing about risks. More often than not, when

149

you close the door on one, you open it for another. All you can really do is try to choose among them in the way that best balances things out overall. This is seldom easy.

With growling and snapping aggression as normal (meaning exhibited by most individuals) as it seems to be, and biting, although much less common, still cropping up in about 15 percent of dogs, it's likely that if we're going to have dogs, we're going to continue to have some dog bites. A very small percentage of those bites will injure.

If we improve our puppy socialization practices, stop using force-based training methods, and stop breeding injuriously biting dogs, we can probably significantly decrease the incidence of growling, snarling, snapping, and biting in dogs. But we're unlikely to eliminate these behaviors. In addition, some dogs will continue to injure people through sheer rambunctiousness. Is it worth it? If my brother could turn back time and take his choice of risks today, I'm pretty sure I know what he'd say.

Allergy reduction alone could easily cancel out the risk to children from dog bites many times over. Asthma, the most severe common manifestation of allergies, afflicts millions of children, with 266 dying of the ailment each year in the US. The Swedish study showed that the likelihood of allergic sensitization was cut in half among children who had lived with at least two dogs or a dog and a cat during the first year of their lives.

The evidence of various health benefits of living with dogs is mounting. It's also important to acknowledge the benefits rendered by dogs with specialized skills from search-and-rescue to assistance for people with disabilities to animal assisted therapy. Such working dogs save significant numbers of human lives and enormously improve the quality of many more. New research with dogs trained to detect various cancers is particularly exciting. Still, it's the day-to-day benefits of sharing our homes with dogs that carry truly large scale illness prevention effects.

Many of the studies of health benefits started out as fishing expeditions. In other words, the researchers were comparing different groups of people on various health measures and collecting all kinds of information about them, in the hopes that something would surface.

Take An Aspirin, Eat Less Fat, And Get A Dog

Several large-scale studies have now documented a correlation between pet ownership and decreased risk of cardiovascular disease, either in terms of lower risk factors for developing disease or of survival rates post heart attack. In one large Australian study (of almost 6,000 people participating in a free heart-health screening clinic) pet owners had significantly lower blood pressure and cholesterol levels than non-pet owners. In men, the difference was comparable to that between those who alter their diets for heart health reasons and those who don't.

Since the benefits of exercise with regard to cardiovascular health are well known, one explanation that has been put forward is that people with dogs may be more likely to engage in healthy moderate exercise by simply walking the dog than are those without pets. There are some data to support this, although probably not enough to account for the difference in heart health.

The research is mixed, one study showing that although more dog owners than non-owners get the recommended amount of exercise for cardiovascular benefit, few of either group actually achieve this. Some studies show dog owners reporting more time spent in vigorous exercise, but others have not found this difference.

Dog ownership does correlates with higher levels of general physical activity, however, even if it doesn't meet the established threshold for cardiovascular conditioning. One study showed an average of 1.4 hours spent outside playing or walking with the dog and simply less sedentary time. This is known to contribute to extending the time older people can spend living independently. Moreover, these differences don't apply only to people who have always had dogs.

Too Many Aches And Pains? Get A Dog

Common health complaints including backaches, headaches, and contracting the flu decreased a few months after adopting a dog or a cat according to a 1991 study in the UK. A more recent 10-month study of three groups of people who began the period with similar reported levels of common minor ailments confirmed the earlier findings. This study was designed to rule out the possibility that people were able to keep dogs because they were already in better health. All the people in the study started out pet-less. One group adopted cats, another dogs, and the last group remained pet-less.

Throughout the 10 months of the study, the new dog owners reported significantly better health than those without pets, and sustained that improvement for longer than the cat owners. The dog owners also reported a dramatic increase in walking that did not occur among the other groups, although, interestingly, the walkers did not separate out as group reporting fewer health problems. The change in overall health and well being seems to be related to dog ownership itself.

Much of this research was sparked when, in 1987, a University of Maryland grad student made the discovery that patients who had pets were surviving heart attacks at a three percent higher rate than those who were isolated. The researcher, Erica Friedman, was testing her hypothesis that a strong social support network enhances the chances of surviving a heart attack for a year. She was able to confirm this, but the connection between pets and heart attack survival was a surprise.

The enhanced survival rate of the pet owners held up even after ruling out the possibility that the survivors exercised more. In order to make sure that it wasn't simply a case of the people who were less sick being more inclined and able to keep pets, Friedman and her colleagues checked for differences in various physiological indicators of cardiovascular risk—and found no significant difference between the patients who owned pets and those who didn't. Nor did the groups differ in terms of personality type based on standard personality inventories.

Another study done in 1994 found that people who do not have pets are at a 30 percent greater risk of dying within six years of having a heart attack than those with pets. The findings with regard to pet ownership and social connection may be related, of course.

Social Life A Little Slow? Walk The Dog

As every dog-park habitué knows, dogs are social magnets. One zoologist in the UK has documented this by observing social encounters in public parks. People walking with dogs had more and longer conversations with other people than those who walked by themselves or even with children. Another British researcher was able to document similar findings when he sent the same individual out with and without a dog. Significantly more people approached and engaged the subject in conversation when he was accompanied by a dog.

All of these findings relate to long term effects of living with pets on general well being and cardiovascular health in particular, which could be at least partly explained in terms of lifestyle changes that frequently accompany pet guardianship. However, it has also been demonstrated that interacting with a pet can directly reduce blood pressure.

Feeling Stressed? Pet Your Dog

In an effort to explain her heart-attack survival findings, the Maryland researcher, Erica Friedman, now at CUNY, has determined that people experiencing very mild stress (talking or reading to a stranger) can lower their blood pressure by talking to their dogs. And the change is impressive, with blood pressure going down to baseline (resting heart rate) levels or even farther.

Another study showed that women waiting for dental procedures—a much higher level of stress—also experience lower blood pressure when their dogs were present. Yet another researcher found that the presence of the subject's dog lowered blood pressure more significantly than did meditation in experienced meditators.

New studies at the University of Missouri offer some possible links to tie both the physiological and emotional threads together. It seems that petting one's dog increases "feel good" neurochemicals, and decreases ones connected with stress. After 15 to 30 minutes of stroking their own dogs, research subjects showed increased levels of serotonin, the same tranquility hormone that was found in elevated levels in the tame Siberian foxes. Increasing serotonin is the main goal of nearly all antidepressant and anti-anxiety medication. The effect was not seen with a robotic or even an unfamiliar dog.

In addition, petting their dogs also increased two other hormones associated with pleasure and tranquility, prolactin and oxytocin. The dog petters experienced decreases in cortisol. This is particularly significant, since cortisol is the main chemical associated with fight or flight responses. Chronically elevated levels of this stress hormone have been tied to all manner of health risks, from high blood pressure to immunosuppressant ailments.

Although no one is suggesting that people suffering from depression throw away their Prozac in favor of spending quality time with the family dog, serious consideration is being directed to encouraging people suffering from anxiety disorders to add doggie cuddle time to their other interventions.

The crucial thing to remember here is that this growing evidence of health benefits of interacting with dogs relate to health issues that affect enormous numbers of people, both in terms of morbidity and mortality. Cardiovascular disease is the cause of 40 percent of all deaths in this country, and costs about $368 billion in direct health costs and lost productivity each year. This means that even very minor effects on tiny percentages of those with cardiovascular disease or those at risk for it have the potential for an enormous effect across the whole society.

You have to wonder how long it will be before people find themselves trying to choose between a reduction in their health insurance premiums because they have a dog and an increase on their homeowners insurance because they have a dog. Discouraging dog ownership, whether through fear of litigation, fear of losing protection from all kinds of liability, or criminalization of ownership of whole categories of dogs could have public health repercussions—repercussions that would make even the direst pronouncements about a "dog-bite epidemic" look trivial.

CHAPTER TEN

A Few Simple Strategies
For Reducing Dog Bites

Ruby, my teeth-clacking red Doberman, seems to enjoy nothing in life so much as sniffing out the scents on foliage, preferably in novel places. I think of it as checking her p-mail, but who knows: So I often take her on leash walks in various parks. I have no idea how many times I have watched in horror as people encourage their toddlers and older children to approach my completely unknown—to them—dog. Some actually shove the tots at her. As it happens, what Ruby will invariably do when in proximity to any human face is lick it, but these people have no way of knowing this. And yet most of the fuss about dog bites is about kids getting bitten.

The simplest, most direct way to decrease the rate of dog bites to children is almost certainly to alter the children's behavior around dogs along with the behavior of the adults who supervise them.

One study of 100 cases of dog bites to children treated in hospitals in Belgium concluded that 67 percent of the bites could have been prevented by modifying the behavior of either the children or adults involved. To explain it another way, quickly read through the following quiz.

1. True or false: Children should be supervised around open bodies of water and swimming pools.
2. True or false: Children should be supervised around open bodies of water and swimming pools even if they've been told not to go in without an adult present.
3. True or false: An adult should have constant eye contact on a swimming or wading child if no other adult is watching.
4. True or false: Children should be prevented from running around wildly on a wet pool deck.
5. True or false: Children should be taught to swim before being allowed in deep water.
6. True or false: Adults supervising swimming children should know how to swim.
7. True or false: Swimming pools are malicious.

Hopefully, you had no difficulty answering these questions. Dogs, obviously, are nowhere nearly as dangerous as bodies of water like lakes and swimming pools. Currently about 1,000 children drown each year in this country compared to around 10 dog-bite victims. Still, if we are serious about reducing the incidence of dog bites to children, we would do well to adopt this motto: If you wouldn't let them do it around a pool, don't let them do it around a dog.

We know what kinds of situations are likely to trigger biting in dogs. They're pretty much the same ones that arouse aggression in humans. They include attacking or threatening the dog, and any stranger approach can seem to be a threat to the undersocialized dog, as can grabbing him in any way. They include taking his stuff or her puppies, and touching him when he's in pain. They include acting like prey. Most of these situation are easy to avoid, and most dogs can even be taught to tolerate them.

A lot could be accomplished by simply heeding a tired old dog-trainers' joke:

Question: *"How do you approach a strange dog?"*
Answer: *"Never."*

We ought to be emblazoning this on billboards. If children are simply taught to ask the owner's permission before interacting with a dog, to let dogs approach them rather than approaching dogs, and to wait to touch a dog until it touches them, neophobically and territorially inspired aggressive behaviors will be largely avoided.

Let Sleeping Dogs Lie

If children are taught not to take food or toys from dogs and not to approach them when they are eating or sleeping, most competitive aggressive responses will be avoided. If children are taught to touch dogs gently, most defensive responses will be avoided. If children are taught not run around or run away from dogs, and especially not to do it while shrieking and flailing in their uncannily accurate imitation of wounded gazelles, most predatory responses will be prevented.

Be A Tree, Not A Bunny

Finally, if children can be taught to stand still and "be a tree" if approached by an unaccompanied unfamiliar dog, even one that's clearly threatening, many of the rare serious attacks can be prevented. It may be strongly counter-intuitive and difficult to freeze in the presence of a scary dog. But this heat-of-the-moment difficulty doesn't stop us from teaching children to drop and roll if their clothes catch fire. It is simply a matter of having them practice a safer alternative behavior to the intuitive running and flailing, which just happens to be the worst possible course of action in cases of fire and dog attack.

Lifeguards Should Know How To Swim

And of course the adults who could impart this information to their kids would do well to heed it themselves. Most adults can easily take it a step farther and learn to recognize basic dog body-language signals of discomfort (turning away, lip licking, yawning, etc.) and not press their attentions on an animal who is exhibiting stress in these ways. It's surprising to me that people need to be taught to avoid a dog that is backing away or growling or standing stiff-legged and not approaching them, but clearly many people need this instruction.

I often wonder in the odd idle moment how many thousands of dog bites would be avoided if people could simply unlearn the idiotic idea that one should stick one's hand in the face of an unknown dog. It's no coincidence that the hands are the most commonly bitten body part on adults.

Once these basic safety precautions are well disseminated, we will begin to be able to judge whether people really care about decreasing dog bites. The fact that childhood drownings have decreased more than 30 percent in the 15 to 20 years since there's been a concerted public information campaign is encouraging. However, it clearly doesn't suggest that kids will ever be rendered completely drown-proof any more than they will become bite-proof.

Some of the improvement in the drowning statistics is probably due to fences being installed around pools and increased use of life jackets. There are analogous things we can do to limit unsupervised access to dogs. Leash laws can be enforced more consistently. More fenced areas can be provided for off-leash dog play. Dogs with histories of damaging bites can be kept strictly confined. Moreover, we can produce safer dogs.

Making Safer Dogs—Better Breeding

It is certainly genetically practical to breed dogs with higher average thresholds for the various triggers for aggression, whether defensive, competitive, territorial, neophobic or even maternal or pain elicited. But it is extremely unlikely that we can transform canines into a species (extremely rare in the animal world) with no aggression triggers at all, i.e., with no means of self defense. Most will probably still resort to warnings and if those don't work, to bites given a strong enough perceived threat. Actions like hitting a cornered dog or snatching away the best food a ravenous one has ever seen are likely to remain dangerous no matter what.

The trick is to figure out the kinds of benign interactions that we want to be able to have with dogs that are now sometimes problematic. We can then breed dogs who actually find those interactions benign. We can produce dogs, for example, who can remain relaxed when people approach them while they eat or snooze in a favorite spot, and when people pat them roughly and groom them and even hug them, and when unfamiliar people enter their homes or approach them on the street. We could probably produce a population of dogs, in short, with less neophobia and more affiliativeness and fewer defensive triggers; dogs that are less inclined to perceive threats in various human postures and actions; dogs who will not take exception when people fail to heed the advice in the previous section. We may even be able to breed dogs with less predatory drive, less inclined to chase rabbits and squirrels and small, shrieking, flailing children.

We don't yet have definitive information about the precise situations in which dogs actually most often warn or bite. We have suspects, of course, like collar grabs and restraint in general, along with sudden stranger approaches, all of which seem to trigger defensive responses in significant numbers of dogs. Some work has been done on this question, largely based on caseload analyses of practitioners who work with large numbers of aggression cases, but much remains to be done.

A good start would be simply spaying and neutering all dogs that bite and injure people, to put forward one possible standard. We'll wind up eliminating from the gene pool some of those who bit in response to pain or beatings or being terrorized or having their food taken away in the face of starvation, but we'll also weed out those who bit in response to more benign situations.

We won't, of course, have any effect on those who threatened— even repeatedly—but did not bite or were restrained from biting. But it's a place to start, and one for which we have the beginnings of the bureaucratic mechanisms in place. We just need all medical professionals who treat dog bites to report them and animal control agencies to follow up with spay and neuter enforcement.

We do need to bear in mind, however, even if we can find the political will and muster the resources to both encourage and enforce wide compliance on any kind of single trait selective breeding program that we, like Balyaev with his Siberian Foxes, are certain to get other traits along for the ride, which we may or may not like. Certainly, many fanciers of upright eared or solid colored breeds are likely to be distressed by floppy ears or piebald coats if such traits were to turn out to be consistently linked to increased friendliness and handleability.

Making Dogs Safer—Better Training

We can breed for dogs for high bite thresholds, but it's important to recognize that the thresholds will never disappear altogether, and that sometimes humans will cross them. So we can also selectively breed dogs that easily learn bite inhibition, the limiting of jaw pressure even when upset enough to bite, as discussed in Chapters Three and Five. It might be possible to breed in this behavior full blown in the way it's been bred into bird dogs. Remember Tracy the Golden Retriever who carried Chipper the parakeet in her mouth unharmed? But it probably makes more sense to simply train this into puppies by the straightforward method used in the kinds of puppy training classes first begun by Dr. Ian Dunbar in the 1980's.

These classes emphasize both socialization and bite inhibition. The puppy is exposed to many people varying in appearance in everything from size and gender to wearing funny hats and walking with unusual gaits, to riding in wheelchairs and carrying all manner of objects. The puppy learns to welcome all these humans as potential playmates and sources of good things in general. Most important, he learns that if he uses too much pressure in his play biting, his (human) playmate will yelp and end the play session. The standard for "too much" pressure is gradually increased until it is no pressure at all.

This training and socialization approach can be used to enhance genetically prepared tolerance. Remember, one of our concerns is with the generalized fear of (and resulting hostility toward) new stuff. So the more kinds of people and situations puppies are exposed to early on, the fewer will actually be new to them when the fear period sets in. The UPS man in his uniform becomes simply "a been there, done that" stimulus to the puppy who has seen many, many uniformed people, instead of the scary monster he may seem to the uninitiated pup.

We can also often prevent dogs from becoming touchy about things like being approached by a person when they're munching on a nice meaty bone. We simply teach the puppy early on that a person approaching usually means she's about to get an extra special treat, rather than lose the treasure she's currently enjoying. We can prevent dogs becoming nervous about children or strangers by teaching them that the appearance of such people reliably predicts "good stuff for dogs," as the famed dog trainer Jean Donaldson likes to refer to it, e.g., games of frisbee and fetch and tug-of-war and yummy treats.

We can even take a behavior like Ruby's teeth clacking and reward it selectively, only when we ask for it, and withdraw our attention when it is offered without the cue. Pretty soon Ruby learns that it doesn't pay to "smile" unless she's heard the magic word. It's not my purpose here, clearly, to provide specific instruction on behavior modification. This has been done quite brilliantly and thoroughly by others. The recommended reading list following this chapter lists my candidates for the best books to guide those who want to take their dogs to an even higher standard of bite proofing than is usual for the species.

There is so much we can do to decrease the number of dog bites to humans. We can educate people, especially children, about the kinds of actions that most often upset dogs enough to cause them to bite. We can eliminate dogs that bite hard enough to injure people from the gene pool. We can train puppies to bite softly so as not to injure humans even when they are upset enough to bite. And we can train dogs, especially if we begin when they are puppies, to be more relaxed in the presence of human actions that might otherwise irritate and frighten them.

These are all laudable goals, and it is my sincere hope that we will make steady progress toward them.

Still, I often reflect on a casual lunch conversation with a group of friends some years ago. We were all education professionals spending our lives working toward worthy, socially constructive goals. The conversation turned to denouncing some commonplace carelessness that sometimes harms people; I don't remember what it was. One among us interrupted with a story. She had had a child fairly late in life and was as fierce in her protection of him as a mother can be. She spoke of chatting with friends on a front porch one pleasant afternoon when her son was a baby. His stroller abruptly began to roll toward the edge of the porch and she was barely able to catch it before it would have fallen over a long drop.

"I realized then," she said, "how everything can change in a moment. It just can."

She explained that what she took from this was that you do your best and hope for the best and try not to waste your short life on fear and blame. Sadly, she didn't live to see her son grow up. She died of one of those ugly, commonplace illnesses that people actually do die of. But I don't think she wasted very much of her time.

Recommended Reading

There are many excellent books available on sound humane methods to use in helping dogs become safe pleasant companions. Here are my candidates for the top three. Any one of these is enough to give you the tools you need. If you want more, they each have their own resource recommendations.

Before and After You Get Your Puppy—Ian Dunbar.
New World Library, 2004.
Everything you need to get your puppy off to a safe happy start.

The Culture Clash—Jean Donaldson.
James & Kenneth Publishers, 1996.
Simply the best book ever written to help people understand dog behavior, with the added bonus   of lots of information on shaping and modifying   that behavior.

Dog Friendly Dog Training—Andrea Arden.
Howell Book House, 2000.
A comprehensive training manual as friendly to human readers as its methods are for dogs.

References

Abrantes, R., 1997. *The Evolution of Canine Social Behaviour.* Wakan Tanka Publishers, Naperville, IL.

Abrantes, R., 1997. *Dog Language, An Encyclopedia of Canine Behaviour.* Wakan Tanka Publishers, Naperville, IL.

A community concern: Who let the dogs out (editorial). 2001, June 24. *San Francisco Chronicle,* C6.

Allen, K. M., 2001. Dog ownership and control of borderline hypertension: A controlled randomized trial. Presented at the *22nd Annual Scientific Sessions of the Society of Behavioral Medicine* in Seattle, WA. March 24, 2001.

Allen K.M., Shykoff B.E., Izzo J.L., 2001. Pet Ownership, but Not ACE Inhibitor Therapy, Blunts Home Blood Pressure Responses to Mental Stress. *Hypertension,* 38:815–820.

Allen K. M., Blascovich J., Tomaka J., Kelsey R.M., 1991. Presence of human friends and pet dogs as moderators of autonomic responses to stress in women. *J. Pers. Soc. Psych.,* 61(4):582–9.

American Kennel Club. Breed registration statistics. Retrieved June 5, 2004 from the AKC web site: http://www..akc.org.

American Horse Council. Horse Industry Statistics. Available from: http://www.horsecouncil.org/ahcstats.html (accessed 10/5/04) Industry Statistics.

American Pet Products Manufacturers Association (APPMA). Fact Sheet. 2003/2004. http://www..appma.org/press_industrytrends.asp (Retrieved January 10, 2004)

Anastasopoulou A., Weiss H.B., Forjuoh S.N., 1998. *Fall Injuries in Pennsylvania.* 1994. Center for Violence and Injury Control (CVIC), Department of Emergency Medicine, Pittsburgh, PA: Allegheny University of the Health Sciences. Retrieved December 19, 2002 from Pennsylvania Department of Health web site: http://www.health.state.pa.us/pdf/php/injprev/falls94.pdf

AVMA Task Force on Canine Aggression and Human-Canine Interactions. A community approach to dog bite prevention. 2001. *JAVMA.,* 218:1732–1749.

Avner, J.R., Baker M.D., 1991. Dog Bites in Urban Children. *Pediatrics,* 88(1):55–57.

Bakker, T.C.M., 1985. Two-way selection for aggression in juvenile, female and male sticklebacks (Gasterosteus aculeatus L.), with some notes on hormonal factors. *Behaviour,* 93:69–81.

Bandow, J.H., Will breed-specific legislation reduce dog bites? 1996. *Can. Vet. J.,* 37, 478–482.

Barker, S., 1999. Therapeutic Aspects of the Human-Companion Animal Interaction. *Psychiatric Times,* 16 (2):45–6

Beck, A.M., Meyers, N.M., 1996. Health enhancement and companion animal ownership, *Annual Review of Public Health,* 17:247–257.

Beck, A.M., Katcher A.H. 1993. *Between Pets and People: The Importance of Animal Companionship.* Revised Edition. Purdue University Press, West Lafayette, IN .

Beck, A.M, Jones B.A. 1985. Unreported dog bites in children. Public Health Rep, 100, 315–321.

Belyaev, D. K., 1979. Destabilizing selection as a factor in domestication. *J. Hered.,* 70:301–308.

Borchelt, P.L., and Voith V.I., 1983. Attacks by packs of dogs involving predation on human beings. *Public Health Rep.,* 98:57–66.

Centers for Disease Control and Prevention (CDC). (2003). Nonfatal Dog Bite--Related Injuries Treated in Hospital Emergency Departments—United States, 2001. *MMWR Morb Mortal Wkly. Rep.,* 52(26):605–610.

CDC. Dog-Bite-Related Fatalities—United States 1995–1996. 1997. *MMWR Morb Mortal Wkly Rep.,* 46:463–467.

Centers for Disease Control and Prevention. Human rabies prevention—United States, 1999. Recommendations of the Advisory Committee on Immunization Practices (ACIP). *MMWR Morb Mortal Wkly. Rep.,* 48(RR-1):1–21.

CDC—WISQARS (Web-based Injury Statistics Query and Reporting System) Online 2003. National Center for Injury Prevention and Control, Centers for Disease Control and Prevention. Available from: www.cdc.gov/ncipc/wisqars. (All data on mortality/morbidity/ED data)

CDC. Injury Fact Book 2001–2002. Available from: http://www.cdc.gov/ncipc/fact_book/factbook.htm#PDF

Coppinger, R., Coppinger, L., 2001. *Dogs: A Startling New Understanding Of Canine Origin, Behavior, And Evolution.* Scribner, New York.

Curran, E.B., Holle, R. L., López, R. E., 1999. Lightning Casualties and Damages in the United States from 1959 to 1994. *Journal of Climate,* 13(9):3448–3464.

Daly, M., Wilson, M., 1988. *Homicide.* Aldine deGruyter, Hawthorne, NY.

Delise, K., 2002. *Fatal Dog Attacks: The Stories Behind The Statistics.* Anubis Press, Manorville, NY.

DENVER, COLO., REV. MUNI. CODE §8–55(a) (2001).

Dire, D.J., 1991. Cat bite wounds: risk factors for infection. *Ann. Emerg. Med.,* 20:973–979

Donaldson, J., 2003. *Mine! A Guide To Resource Guarding In Dogs.* Kinship Communications/SF-SPCA, San Francsicso, CA.

DTI, (U.K. Department of Trade and Industry) 1996. Fatal Drowning Accidents—5 Gallon Buckets. *DTI,* March 1996.

Favre, D. S., & Borchelt, P.L., 1999. *Animal Law and Dog Behavior.* Lawyers & Judges Pub. Co., Tuscon, AZ.

Friedmann, E., 1995. The role of pets in enhancing human well-being: Physiological effects. In I. Robinson (Ed.), *The Waltham Book Of Human-Animal Interaction: Benefits And Responsibilities Of Pet Ownership* (pp.33–53). Pergamon, Oxford, England.

Friedmann E., Thomas, S.A., 1995. Pet Ownership, Social Support, and One-Year Survival After Acute Myocardial Infarction in the Cardiac Arrhythmia Suppression Trial (CAST). *Am. J. Cardiol.,* 76:1213–1217

Furber, S., 1998. Effects of companion animals on the quality of life of older people: A critical review and research agenda. *Proceedings of Animals, Community Health and Public Policy Symposium.* Sydney, Australia.

Fremont Boy, Four, Attacked By Pit Bull, April 20, 2003. *San Francisco Chronicle,* A26.

Gaffney, P., 2000. The domestic iron. A danger to young children. *J. Accid. Emerg. Med.,* 17(3):199–200.

Gathright, A., February 6, 2001. Pit Bull Bites Three Boys: Is shot Dead. *San Francisco Chronicle,* A13.

Gershman, K.A, Sacks., J.J., Wright, J.C., 1994. Which Dogs Bite? A Case Control Study of Risk Factors. *Pediatrics,* 93(6):913–916.

Gigerenzer, G., 2002. *Calculated Risks: How to Know when Numbers Deceive You.* Simon & Schuster, New York, NY.

Glassner, Barry., 1999. *The Culture of Fear: Why Americans Are Afraid of The Wrong Things.* Basic Books, New York, NY.

Goodloe, L.P., and Borchelt, P.L., 1998. Companion dog temperament traits. *J. Appl. Anim. Welfare. Sci.,* 1:303–338.

Griego, R.D., Rosen, T., Orengo, I.F., Wolf, J.E., 1995. Dog, cat, and human bites: a review. *J. Am. Acad. Dermatol.,* 33:1019–1029.

Gulevich, R.G., Oskina, I.N., Shikhevich, S.G., Fedorova, E.V., Trut, L.N., 2004. Effect of selection for behavior on pituitary-adrenal axis and propiomelanocortin gene expression in silver foxes *(Vulpes vulpes)*. *Physiol. Behav.*, 82(2–3):513–8.

Guy, N. C., *et al.*, 2001. Demographic and aggressive characteristics of dogs in a general veterinary caseload. *Applied Animal Behaviour Science*, 74(1):15–28.

Guy, N. C., Luescher, U.A., *et al.*, 2001. Risk factors for dog bites to owners in a general veterinary caseload. *Applied Animal Behaviour Science*, 74(1):29–42.

Guy, N. C., Luescher U.A., *et al.*, 2001. A case series of biting dogs: Characteristics of dogs, their behaviour, and their victims. *Applied Animal Behaviour Science*, 72(4):43–57.

Haltom, W., and McCann, M., 2004. *Distorting the Law: Politics, Media, and the Litigation Crisis.* Univ. of Chicago Press, Chicago, IL.

Hayward, G., 1996. Risk of injury per hour of exposure to consumer products. *Accident Analysis & Prevention*, 28(1):115–121

Headey, B., 2003 Editorial: Pet ownership: good for health? *M.J.A.*, 179(9):460–461.

Headey, B., Grabka, M., Kelley, J., *et al.*, 2002. Pet ownership is good for your health and saves public expenditure too: Australian and German longitudinal evidence. *Aust. Social. Monitor.*, 4:93–99.

Hensler, D.R., *et.al.*, 1991. *Compensation for Accidental Injuries in the United States.* Rand, Santa Monica, CA.

Hesselmar, B., Aberg, N., Aberg, B., Eriksson, B., Borksten, B., 1999. Does early exposure to cat or dog protect against later allergy development? Department of Pediatrics, University of Goteborg, Goteborg, Sweden. *Clinical Exp. Allergy*, 29(5):611–7.

Horseback-Riding-Associated Traumatic Brain Injuries— Oklahoma (1992-1994), 1996. *MMWR Morb. Mortal. Wkly. Rep.*, 45(10):209–211.

III., (Insurance Information Institute) *Dog Bite Liability.* Accessed 11/13/04 from: http://www.iii.org/media/hottopics/insurance/dogbite/

III., *Facts and Statistics: Homeowners Insurance.* Available from: URL: http://www.iii.org/media/facts/statsbyissue/homeowners/ [accessed11/20/04]

Introduction to the Caucasian Ovcharka, United States Caucasian Ovcharka Preservation Society. Accessed 6/25/04 from: http://www.ovcharka-breeds.com/THC1.htm

Jumbelic, M.I., Chambliss, M., 1990. Accidental toddler drowning in 5–gallon buckets. *J.A.M.A.*, 263(14):1952–3.

Kahn, A., Bauche, P., Lamoureux, J., 2003. Child victims of dog bites treated in emergency departments: a prospective survey. *Eur. J. Pediatr.*, 162(4):254–8.

Kingwell, B.A., Lomdahl, A., Anderson, W.P., 2001. Presence of a pet dog and human cardiovascular responses to mild mental stress. *Clin. Auton. Res.*, 11:313–317.

Klaassen, B., Buckley, J.R., Esmail, A,. 1996. Does the Dangerous Dogs Act protect against animal attacks: a prospective study of mammalian bites in the accident and emergency department. *Injury*, 27(2):89–91.

Kochanek, K., Murphy, S.L., Anderson, R.N., Scott, C., 2004. Deaths: Final Data for *2002 National Vital Statistics Reports* 53(5):1–116.

Krebs, J.W., Rupprecht, C.E., Childs, J.E., 2000. Rabies surveillance in the United States during 1999. *J. Am. Vet. Med. Assoc.*, 217(12):799–811.

Kulikov, A.V., Zhanaeva, EIu., Popova, N.K., 1989. Change in tryptophan hydroxylase activity in the brain of silver foxes and wild Norway rats in the course of selection according to behavior. (Article in Russian) *Genetika*, 25(2):346-50. Abstract retrieved September 2, 2002, from PubMed database

LeDoux, J., 1996. The Emotional Brain. Touchstone, New York, NY.

Leshner, A. I., 1978. *An Introduction to Behavioral Endocrinology.* Oxford Univ. Press, New York, NY.

Lightning-Associated Deaths—United States (1980-1995), 1998. *MMWR Morb. Mortal. Wkly. Rep.*, 47(19):391–394

Lindsay, S.R., 2001. *Handbook Of Applied Dog Training And Behavior.* (2 vols.) Iowa State University Press, Ames, IA.

Lockwood, R., Rindy, K., 1987. Are "Pit Bulls" different? An Analysis of the Pit Bull Terrier Controversy. *Anthrozoos*, I(1):2–8.

Logan, P., Branche, C.M., Sacks, J.J., Ryan, G., Peddicord, J., 1998. Childhood drownings and fencing of outdoor pools in the United States (1994). *Pediatrics*, 101(6):E3

McNicholas, J., Collis, G.M., 2000. Dogs as catalysts for social interactions: Robustness of the effect. *British J.Psych.*, 91:61–74

Messent, P. R., 1983. Social facilitation of contact with other people by pet dogs. In A. H. Katcher & A. M. Beck (Eds.), *New Perspectives On Our Lives With Companion Animals* (pp. 37-46). University of Philadelphia Press, Philadelphia, PA.

Moore, D.A., Sischo, W.M., Hunter, A., Miles, T., 2000. Animal bite epidemiology and surveillance for rabies postexposure prophylaxis. *J. Am. Vet. Med. Assoc.* 217(2):190–4.

Naumenko, E.V., Popova, N.K., 1989. Behavior, adrenocortical activity and brain monoamines in norway rats selected for reduced aggressiveness towards man. *Pharmacol. Biochem. Behav.,* 33:85–91.

News in brief from the San Francisco Bay Area, Monday, April 21, 2003. *Associated Press State & Local Wire.* Retrieved July 21, 2003, from Lexis-Nexis Academic Index.

News in brief from the San Francisco Bay Area, Monday, April 22, 2003. *Associated Press State & Local Wire.* Retrieved July 21, 2003, from Lexis-Nexis Academic Index.

News in brief from the San Francisco Bay Area, Monday, April 23, 2003. *Associated Press State & Local Wire.* Retrieved July 21, 2003, from Lexis-Nexis Academic Index.

NYC Administrative Code §17–342(definitions) (2000).

Nikulina, E.M., 1991. Neural control of predatory aggression in wild and domesticated animals. *Neurosci. Biobehav. Rev.* 15:545–547.

Nonfatal dog bite-related injuries treated in hospital emergency departments—United States (2001), 2003. *MMWR Morb. Mortal. Wkly. Rep.,* 52(26):605–10

Nonfatal sports- and recreation-related injuries treated in emergency departments—United States (July 2000-June 2001), 2002. *MMWR Morb. Mortal. Wkly. Rep.,* 51(33):736–40.

Rönmark, E., Perzanowski, M., Platts-Mills, T., Lundbäck, B., 2003. Four-year incidence of allergic sensitization among schoolchildren in a community where allergy to cat and dog dominates sensitization: Report from the Obstructive Lung Disease in Northern Sweden Study Group. *Journal of Allergy and Clinical Immunology,* 112(4):747–754.

Odendaal, J.S., Meintjes, R.A., 2003. Neurophysiological Correlates of Affiliative Behavior Between Humans and Dogs. *Vet. J.,* 165:296–301.

Oswald, M., 1991. Report on the Potentially Dangerous Dog Program: Multnomah County, Oregon. *Anthrozoos,* 5(4):247–54.

Ownby, D.R., Johnson, C.C., Peterson, E.L., 2002. Exposure to dogs and cats in the first year of life and risk of allergic sensitization at 6 to 7 years of age. *J.A.M.A.,* 288(8):963–72.

Ozanne-Smith, J., Ashby, K., Stathakis, V,. 1998. Dog bites and injury prevention—a critical review and research agenda. *Proceedings of Animals, Community Health and Public Policy Symposium.* Sydney, Australia.

Parker, H.G., Kim, L.V., *et.al.* 2004. Genetic Structure of the Purebred Domestic Dog. *Science,* 304:1160–64.

Plyusnina, I., Oskina, I., 1997. Behavioral and adrenocortical responses to open-field test in rats selected for reduced aggressiveness toward humans. *Physiology & Behavior,* 61(3):381–385.

Popova, N., Voitenko, N., Kulikov, A., Avgustinovich, D., 1991. Evidence for the involvement of central serotonin in mechanism of domestication of silver foxes. *Pharmacol. Biochem. Behav.,* 40:751–756.

Popova, N.K., Avgustinovich, D.F., Kolpakov, V.G., Plyusnina, I.Z., 1998. Specific [3H]8-OH-DPAT binding in brain regions of rats genetically predisposed to various defense behavior strategies. *Pharmacol. Biochem. Behav.,* 59(4):793–7 Abstract retrieved October 24, 2001, from PubMed database.

Quinlan, K.P., Sacks, J.J., 1999. Hospitalizations for dog bite injuries (letter). *J.A.M.A.,* 281:232–233.

Raina, P., Waltner-Toews, D., Bonnett, B., Woodward, C., Abernathy, T., 1999. Influence of companion animals on the physical and psychological health of older people: an analysis of a one-year longitudinal study. *J. Am. Geriatr. Soc.,* 47(3):323–9.

Randolph, M., 2001. *Dog Law.* (4th ed.) Nolo, Berkeley, CA.

Ropeik, D., & Gray, G., 2002. *Risk: A Practical Guide for Deciding What's Really Safe and What's Really Dangerous in the World Around You.* Houghton Mifflin, Boston, MA.

Royal Society for the Prevention of Accidents. Home and Leisure Accident Surveillance System—Annual Report, 2000-2002. Retrieved June 10, 2004 from the ROSPA website at: http://www.rospa.com/hassandlass/reports/2002data.pdf

Sacks, J.J., Kresnow, M., Houston, B., 1996. Dog bites: how big a problem? *Injury Prevention,* 2:52–54.

Sacks, J.J., Sattin, R.W., Bonzo, S.E., 1989. Dog bite-related fatalities from 1979 through 1988. *J.A.M.A.,* 262:1489–1492.

Sacks, J.J., Sinclair, L., Gilchrist, J., Golab, G.C., Lockwood, R., 2000. Breeds of dogs involved in fatal human attacks in the United States between 1979 and 1998. *J.A.V.M.A.,* 217:836–840.

Sacks, J.J., Lockwood, R., Hornreich, J., Sattin, R.W., 1996. Fatal dog attacks (1989-1994). *Pediatrics,* 97, 891–5.

Scott, J.P., Fuller, J.L., 1965. *Genetics and The Social Behavior of The Dog.* Univ. of Chicago Press, Chicago, IL.

Serpell, J.A.,1990. Evidence for long-term effects of pet-ownership on human health. In L.H. Burger (Ed.), *Pets, Benefits and Practice* (pp.1-7). BVA Publications, London, England.

Serpell, J., 1991. Beneficial effects of pet ownership on some aspects of human health and behavior. *J. Royal Soc. Med.,* 84:717–720. Abstract retrieved September 12, 2003, from PubMed database.

Serpell, J., Ed. 1995. *The Domestic Dog.* Cambridge Univ. Press, Cambridge, England.

Shyan, M.R., Fortune, K.A., King, C., 2003. Bark parks—a study on interdog aggression in a limited-control environment. *J. Applied Animal Welfare Science,* 6(1):25–32.

Sosin, D.M., Sacks, J.J., Sattin, R.W., 1992. Causes of non-fatal injuries in the United States (1986). *Accident Analysis and Prevention,* 24:685–687.

Squatriglia, C., Lee, H.K., 2001, January 31. Woman badly hurt in another dog attack. *San Francisco Chronicle,* A16.

Strotmeyer, S.J., Forjuoh, S.N., Coben, J.H., 1999. Dog Bite Injuries in Pennsylvania (1995). Pittsburgh,Pennsylvania: Center for Violence and Injury Control (CVIC), Department of Emergency Medicine, Allegheny University of the Health Sciences. Retrieved on December 12, 2002, from the Pennsylvania Department of Health website: http://www.dsf.health.state.pa.us/health/lib/health/old_dir/pdf/php/injprev/dogbite.pdf.

Suffocations in Grain Bins—Minnesota (1992-1995), 1996. *MMWR Morb. Mortal. Wkly. Rep.,* 45(39):837–841.

Sward, S., 2001, March 18. SF Police Shoot Pit Bull. *San Francisco Chronicle,* A17.

Sylwester, R., 1997. The neurobiology of self-esteem and aggression. *Educational Leadership,* 54:75–9.

Talan, D.A., Citron, D.M., Abrahamian, F.M., 1999. Bacteriologic analysis of infected dog and cat bites. *N. Engl. J. Med.,* 2:85–92.

Tarrago, S.B., 2000. Prevention of choking, strangulation, and suffocation in childhood. *W.M.J.,* 99(9):43–6.

Tinsworth, D., McDonald, J., 2001. Special study. Injuries and deaths associated with children's playground equipment. U.S. Consumer Product Safety Commission.

Trut, L. N., 1996. Sex ratio in silver foxes: effects of domestication and the star gene. *Theoret. Appl. Genet.,* 92:109–115.

Trut, L. N., 1999. Early canid domestication: the farm-fox experiment. *Amer. Sci.,* 87:160–168.

Voith, V.L., Borchelt, P.L., Eds., 1996. *Readings in Companion Animal Behavior.* Veterinary Learning Systems, Trenton, NJ.

Vormbrock, J.K., Grossberg, J.M., 1988. Cardiovascular effects of human-pet dog interactions. *J. Behav. Med.,* 11:509–517 Abstract retrieved June 5, 2003, from PubMed database

Weiss, H.B., Friedman, D.I., Coben, J.H., 1998. Incidence of dog bite injuries treated in emergency departments. *J.A.M.A.,* 279(1):51–53.

Wilks, K., 1999. When dogs are man's best friend — the health benefits of companion animals in the modern society. *Proceedings of Urban animal management conferences in Australia: Dog related subjects.*

Williams, H., Pembroke, A., 1989. Sniffer dogs in the melanoma clinic? *Lancet,* 1:734.

Willis, C.M., Church, S.M., Guest, C.M., Cook, W.A., McCarthy, N., Bransbury A.J., *et. al.* 2004. Olfactory detection of human bladder cancer by dogs: proof of principle study. *B.M.J.,* 329:712.

Wilson, E.O.. 1975. *Sociobiology: The New Synthesis.* Harvard University Press, Cambridge, MA.

Wright, J. C., 1985. Severe attacks by dogs: characteristics of the dogs, the victims, and the attack settings. *Public Health Rep.,* 100:55–61.

Wright, J. C., 1990. Reported cat bites in Dallas: characteristics of the cats, the victims, and the attack events. *Public Health Rep.,* 105:420–424.

The Culture Clash Jean Donaldson

The Culture Clash is utterly unique, fascinating to the extreme, and literally overflowing with information so new that it virtually redefines the state of the art in dog behavior and training. *The Culture Clash* depicts dogs as they really are—stripped of their Hollywood fluff, with their loveable "can I eat it, chew it, urinate on it, what's in it for me" philosophy. The author's tremendous affection for dogs shines through at all times, as does her keen insight into the dog's mind. Relentlessly Jean Donaldson champions the dog's point of view, always showing concern for their education and well-being.

Winner of the Maxwell Award for BEST DOG TRAINING BOOK (1997) from the Dog Writers' Association of America. Voted #1 BEST BOOK (2000 & 2001) by the Association of Pet Dog Trainers

How to Teach A New Dog Old Tricks   Dr. Ian Dunbar

"*How To Teach A New Dog Old Tricks* is the best book by dog training's leading genius. The most relevant, important piece ever written on the subject of dog behavior and training. Some fields are lucky enough to be granted a giant: a figure whose contributions inspire awe and are unsurpassable. Ian Dunbar is that in dog behavior. There is no single person on the face of the planet to whom dog trainers and owners (not to mention dogs) owe more."

Jean Donaldson (author of *The Culture Clash*)

The definitive text for lure/reward training—written from the dog's point of view and emphasizing natural motivational methods to teach your dog to *want* to do what you want him to do! Fun training with toys, treats, lures, and rewards. Easy, fun-loving, methods for teaching a new puppy old tricks (such as basic manners), or for teaching an older dog who is new to training. Voted the #1 BEST BOOK by the Association of Pet Dog Trainers (1999).

Excel-erated Learning Dr. Pamela Reid

At long last we have someone who can explain all-important learning theory and make it intriguing and interesting. Agility enthusiast, obedience competitor and psychologist Dr. Pamela Reid introduces you to cutting-edge scientific techniques in dog training including, autoshaping retrieval (i.e., teaching the dog train himself), and "errorless discrimination learning." You'll just love this book—so useful and utterly fascinating. With the freedom of understanding "how your dog learns" comes the ability of making the process easy, efficient and enjoyable for your dog.

Excel-*erated Learning* has become the textbook of choice for professional trainers who want to learn how to efficiently and effectively change the behavior of dogs, other animals, and people.

Good Little Dog Book Dr. Ian Dunbar

Welcome back to the historically-proven, so-old-that-it's-new-again, natural, common-sense, easy and enjoyable way to train your dog—off-leash, lure/reward, fun and games, dog-friendly dog training. This little book contains helpful hints for socialization, temperament training and behavior modification as well as tips for teaching basic manners.

Dr. Dunbar's training techniques are altogether quicker, easier, gentler, more effective, and certainly considerably more enjoyable for you and your dog. Lure/reward training techniques work like a treat!

Our best friend—the domestic dog—is a social animal. It would be unfair and antisocial not to train him. How else could we communicate? By tail wags and ear positions? Luckily, dogs can easily learn our language...if we teach them! Basically, training comprises teaching dogs ESL (English as a Second Language) so dogs can understand human words for doggy behaviors and actions.

James & Kenneth Publishers

James & Kenneth is just a small puppy publisher, trying to run with the big dogs. However, according to the Association of Pet Dog Trainers—the largest and most influential worldwide association of professional pet dog trainers—we publish some pretty good books and videos. Each year, APDT members vote more James & Kenneth titles to their Top Ten Lists of *Best Books* and *Best Videos for Dog Owners,* than titles from any other book or video publisher.

We are proud to publish Dr. Pamela Reid's classic learning theory text—Excel-*erated Learning,* Jean Donaldson's best-selling *Culture Clash,* and most of Dr. Ian Dunbar's books and videos.

Solutions to common puppy/dog behavior and training problems plus one of Dr. Dunbar's books *BEFORE You Get Your Puppy* are available as free pdf downloads from our website:

www.jamesandkenneth.com